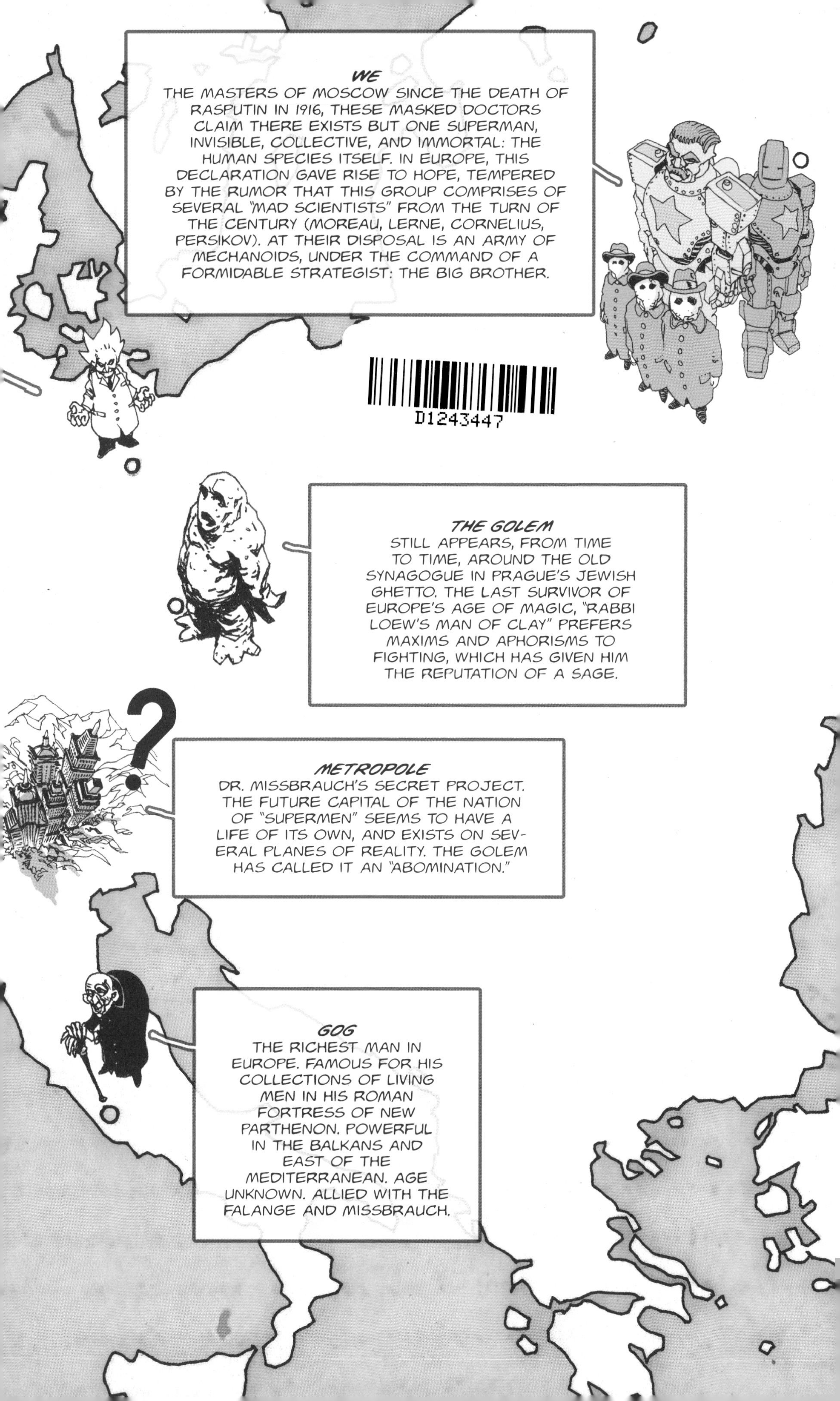
WE
THE MASTERS OF MOSCOW SINCE THE DEATH OF RASPUTIN IN 1916, THESE MASKED DOCTORS CLAIM THERE EXISTS BUT ONE SUPERMAN, INVISIBLE, COLLECTIVE, AND IMMORTAL: THE HUMAN SPECIES ITSELF. IN EUROPE, THIS DECLARATION GAVE RISE TO HOPE, TEMPERED BY THE RUMOR THAT THIS GROUP COMPRISES OF SEVERAL "MAD SCIENTISTS" FROM THE TURN OF THE CENTURY (MOREAU, LERNE, CORNELIUS, PERSIKOV). AT THEIR DISPOSAL IS AN ARMY OF MECHANOIDS, UNDER THE COMMAND OF A FORMIDABLE STRATEGIST: THE BIG BROTHER.
THE GOLEM
STILL APPEARS, FROM TIME TO TIME, AROUND THE OLD SYNAGOGUE IN PRAGUE'S JEWISH GHETTO. THE LAST SURVIVOR OF EUROPE'S AGE OF MAGIC, "RABBI LOEW'S MAN OF CLAY" PREFERS MAXIMS AND APHORISMS TO FIGHTING, WHICH HAS GIVEN HIM THE REPUTATION OF A SAGE.
METROPOLE
DR. MISSBRAUCH'S SECRET PROJECT. THE FUTURE CAPITAL OF THE NATION OF "SUPERMEN" SEEMS TO HAVE A LIFE OF ITS OWN, AND EXISTS ON SEVERAL PLANES OF REALITY. THE GOLEM HAS CALLED IT AN "ABOMINATION."
GOG
THE RICHEST MAN IN EUROPE. FAMOUS FOR HIS COLLECTIONS OF LIVING MEN IN HIS ROMAN FORTRESS OF NEW PARTHENON. POWERFUL IN THE BALKANS AND EAST OF THE MEDITERRANEAN. AGE UNKNOWN. ALLIED WITH THE FALANGE AND MISSBRAUCH.

THE CHIMERA BRIGADE

VOLUME 1

SERGE LEHMAN / FABRICE COLIN /
GESS / CELINE BESSONNEAU

THE CHIMERA BRIGADE

PROLOGUE:
MECANO-CURIE

EPISODE ONE:
THE FINAL MISSION OF THE MAN WHO WALKS THROUGH WALLS

SCRIPT
SERGE LEHMAN
FABRICE COLIN

ART
GESS

COLORS
CELINE BESSONNEAU

TRANSLATION
EDWARD GAUVIN

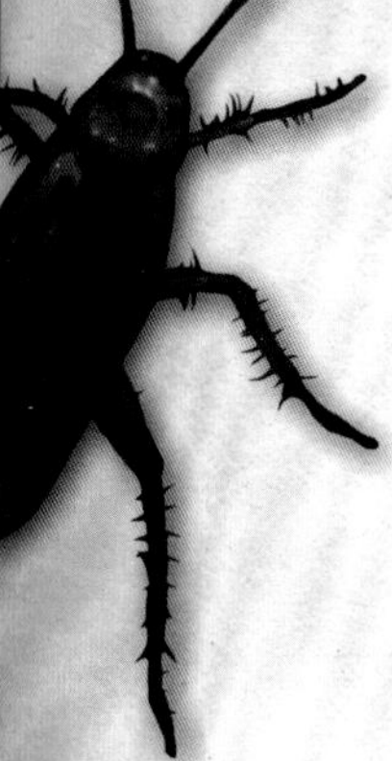

LETTERING
GABRIELA HOUSTON

COVER
MAX BERTOLINI

COVER COLORS
HI-FI COLOUR DESIGN

To Tim, my superhero.
Gess

For J. H. Rosny, H.G. Wells, Jean de La Hire,
Evgueni Zamiatine, Fritz Lang, Giovanni Papini, Jean Ray,
Régis Messac, and all the old guard of the Hyperworld
Serge Lehman

WWW.TITAN-COMICS.COM
@COMICSTITAN
facebook.com/comicstitan

What did you think of this book?
We love to hear from our readers. Please email us at:
readercomments@titanemail.com,
or write to us at the above address.

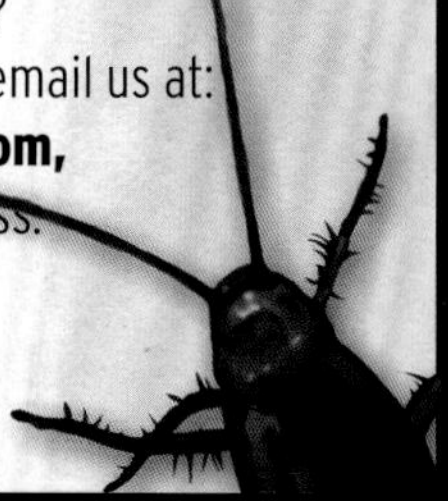

TITAN COMICS

CHIMERA BRIGADE VOLUME 1:
ISBN: 9781782760993

Collection Editor
Gabriela Houston

Collection Designer
Tom Hunt

Senior Editor
Steve White

Titan Comics Editorial
Andrew James, Tom Williams

Production Manager
Obi Onuora

Production Supervisor
Jackie Flook

Production Assistant
Peter James

Art Director
Oz Browne

Studio Manager
Selina Juneja

Circulation Manager
Steve Tothill

Marketing Manager
Ricky Claydon

Senior Marketing and Press Executive
Owen Johnson

Publishing Manager
Darryl Tothill

Publishing Director
Chris Teather

Operations Director
Leigh Baulch

Executive Director
Vivian Cheung

Publisher
Nick Landau

Published by Titan Comics
A division of Titan Publishing Group Ltd.
144 Southwark St.
London, SE1 0UP

A CIP catalogue record for this title is available from the British Library.

First edition: January 2015

Originally published in 2009 by Librairie L'Atalante, France as La Brigade Chimeri

10 9 8 7 6 5 4 3 2 1

Printed in China.
Titan Comics. TC0177

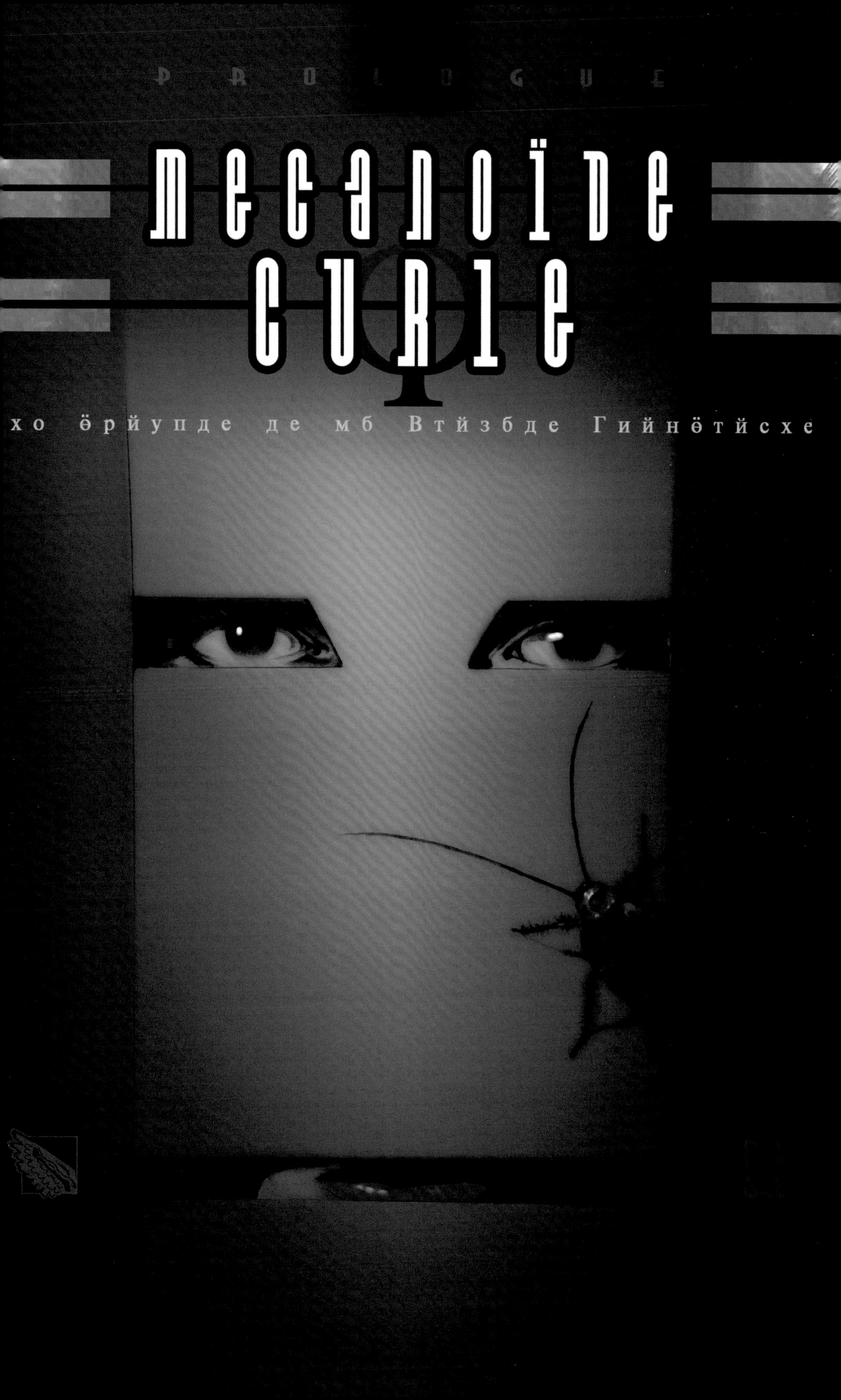
PROLOGUE
MEGALOÏDE CURIE
хо ёрйупде де мб Втйзбде Гийнётйсхе

G E W A L T

DER
KULT
ZUR
MACHT

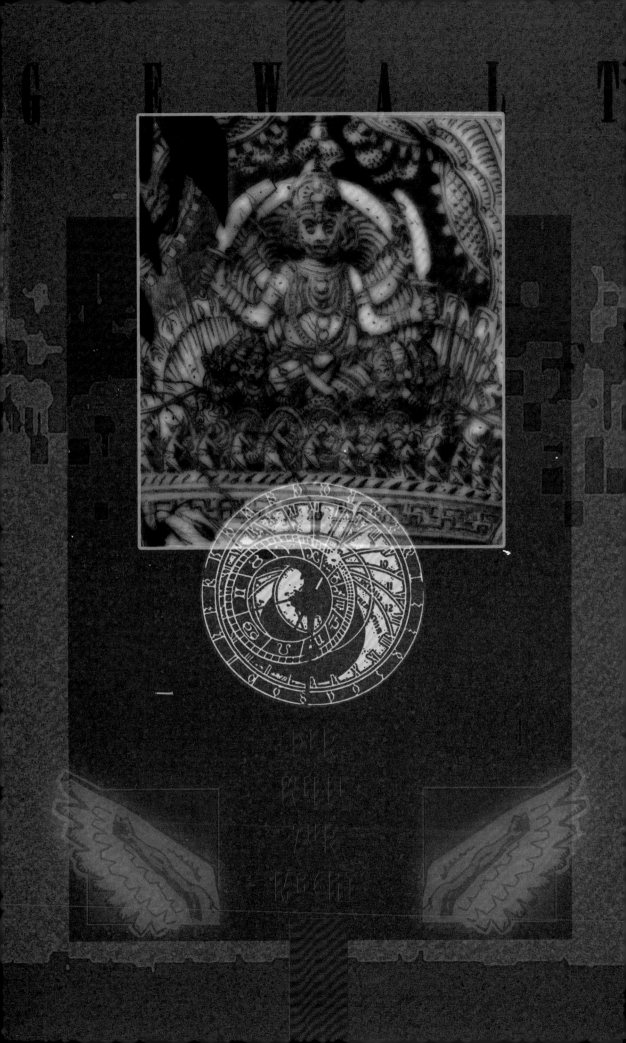

The sublime one saw I today...

...The solemn one, the penitent of spirit: Oh, how my soul _laughed_ at his ugliness!

O'erhung with ugly truths, the spoils of his hunts, and rich in torn raiment; many _thorns_ also hung on him...

...but no _roses_ did I see.

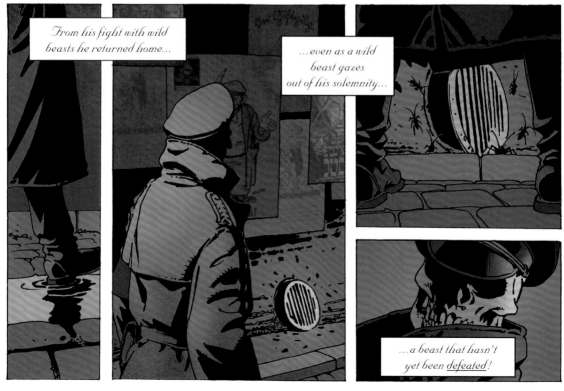

From his fight with wild beasts he returned home...

...even as a wild beast gazes out of his solemnity...

...a beast that hasn't yet been _defeated_!

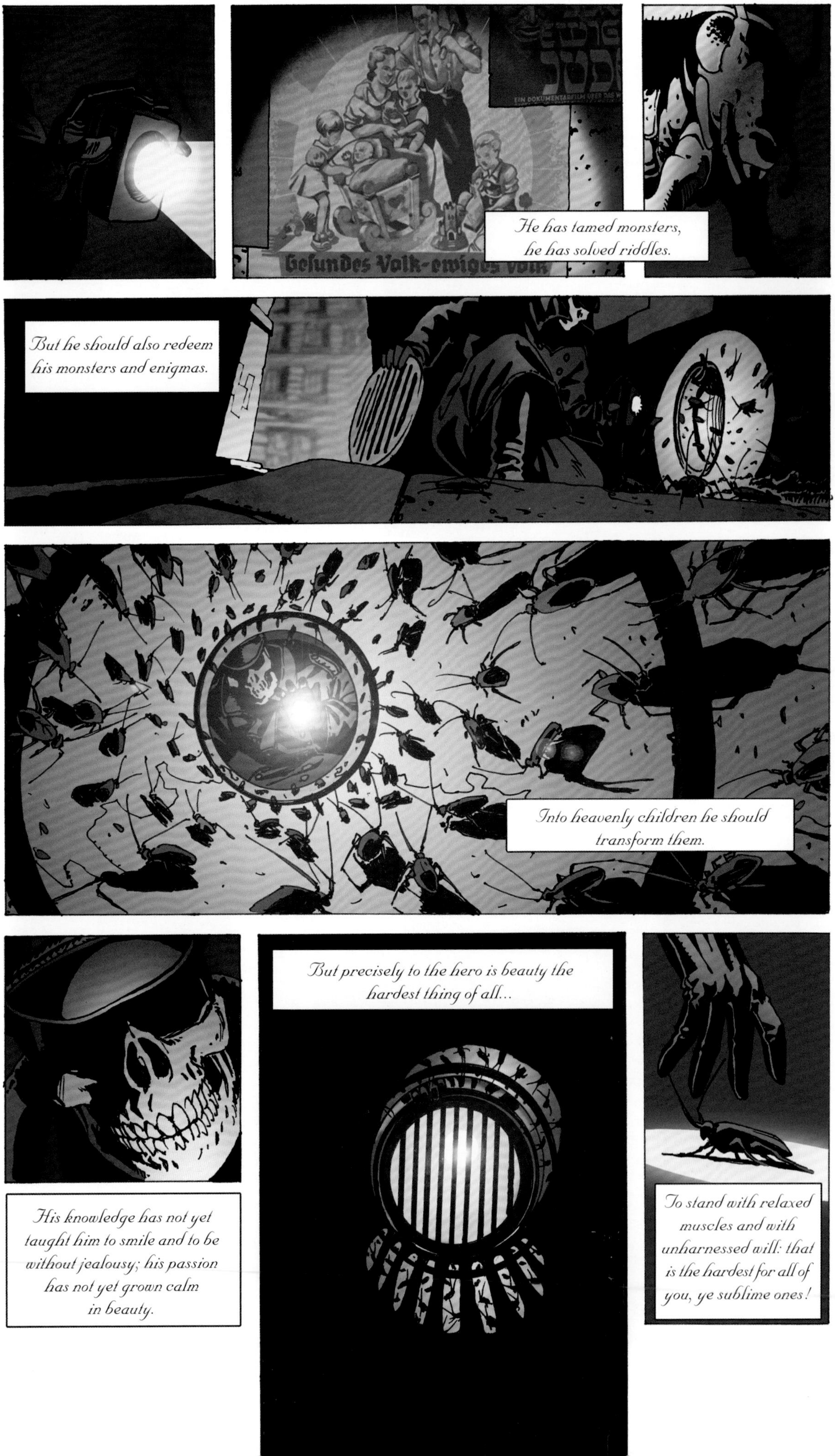
Gesundes Volk-ewiges Volk
He has tamed monsters, he has solved riddles.
But he should also redeem his monsters and enigmas.
Into heavenly children he should transform them.
His knowledge has not yet taught him to smile and to be without jealousy; his passion has not yet grown calm in beauty.
But precisely to the hero is beauty the hardest thing of all...
To stand with relaxed muscles and with unharnessed will: that is the hardest for all of you, ye sublime ones!

And yet, sublime man, you too shall one day be fair and hold the mirror up to your own face...

...then your soul will _shudder_ at its own desires.

And there will be _adoration_ even in your vanity!

For this is the secret of the soul.

Only when the hero has abandoned it...

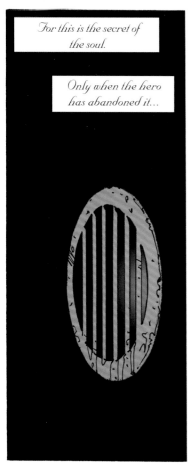

...does he approach in his dreams...

...the superhero.*

* NIETZSCHE, THUS SPAKE ZARATHRUSTRA

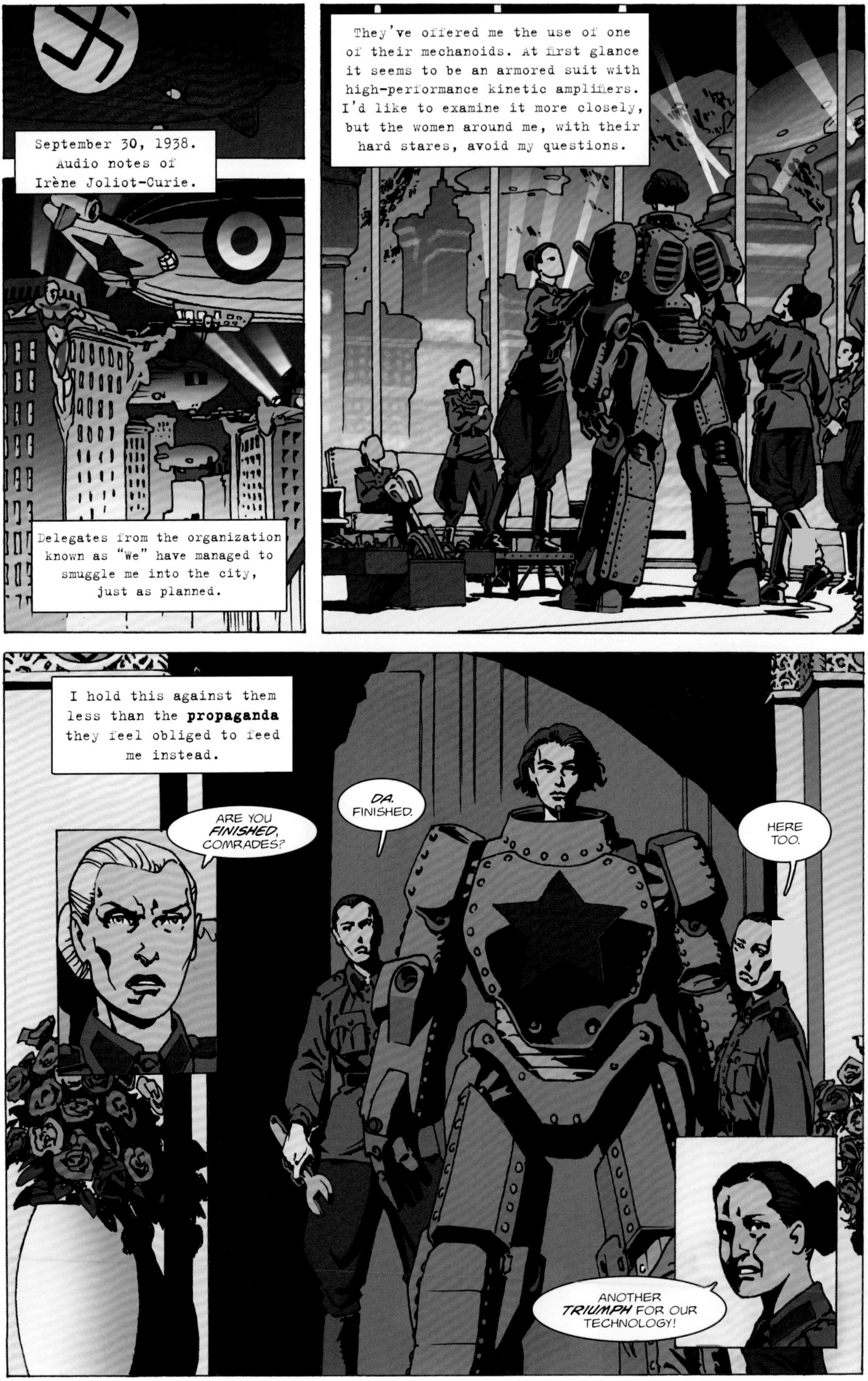
September 30, 1938.
Audio notes of
Irène Joliot-Curie.
Delegates from the organization known as "We" have managed to smuggle me into the city, just as planned.
They've offered me the use of one of their mechanoids. At first glance it seems to be an armored suit with high-performance kinetic amplifiers. I'd like to examine it more closely, but the women around me, with their hard stares, avoid my questions.
I hold this against them less than the **propaganda** they feel obliged to feed me instead.
ARE YOU *FINISHED*, COMRADES?
DA. FINISHED.
HERE TOO.
ANOTHER *TRIUMPH* FOR OUR TECHNOLOGY!

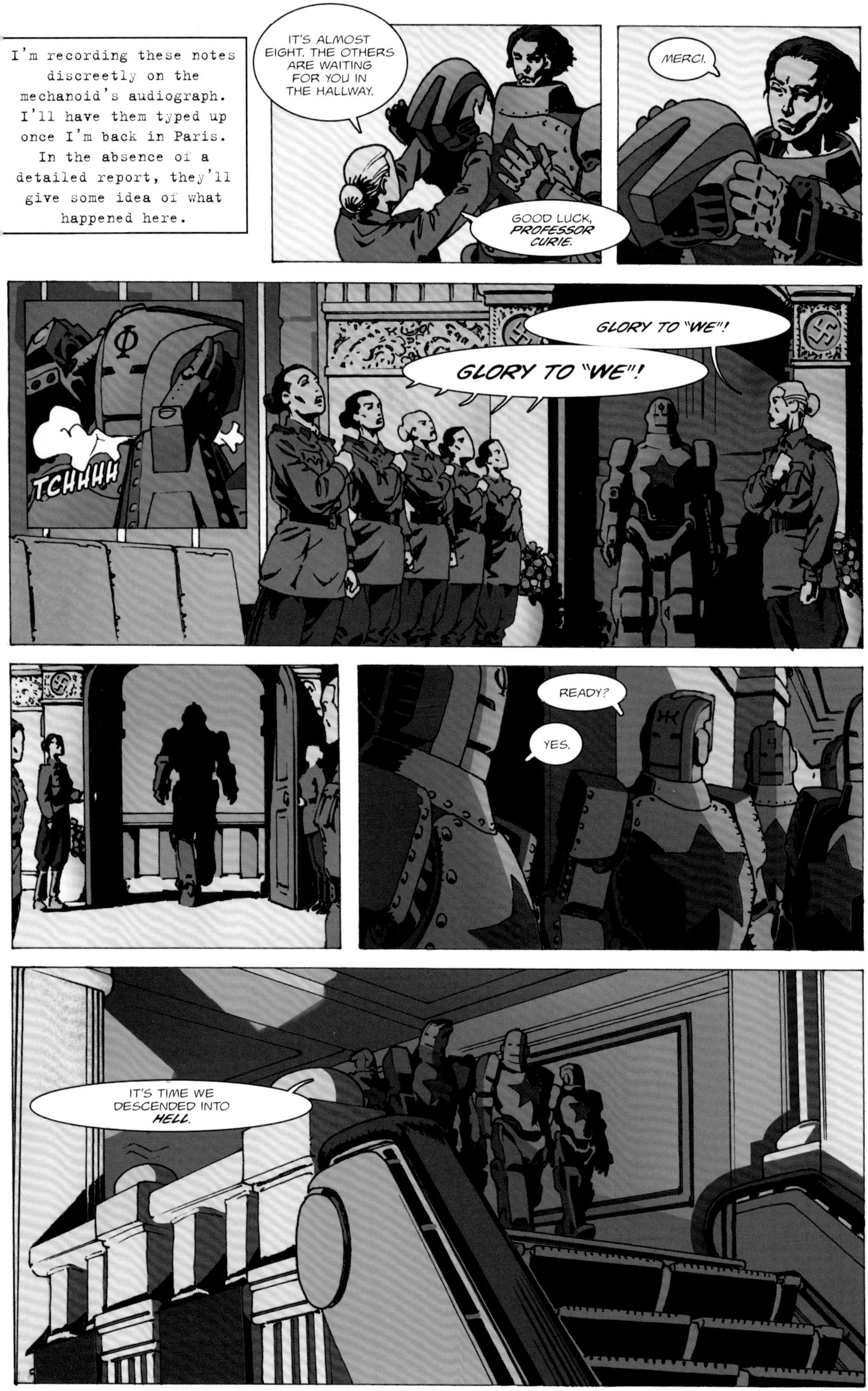

I'm recording these notes discreetly on the mechanoid's audiograph. I'll have them typed up once I'm back in Paris. In the absence of a detailed report, they'll give some idea of what happened here.
IT'S ALMOST EIGHT. THE OTHERS ARE WAITING FOR YOU IN THE HALLWAY.
GOOD LUCK, *PROFESSOR CURIE.*
MERCI.
TCHHHH
GLORY TO "WE"!
GLORY TO "WE"!
READY?
YES.
IT'S TIME WE DESCENDED INTO *HELL*.

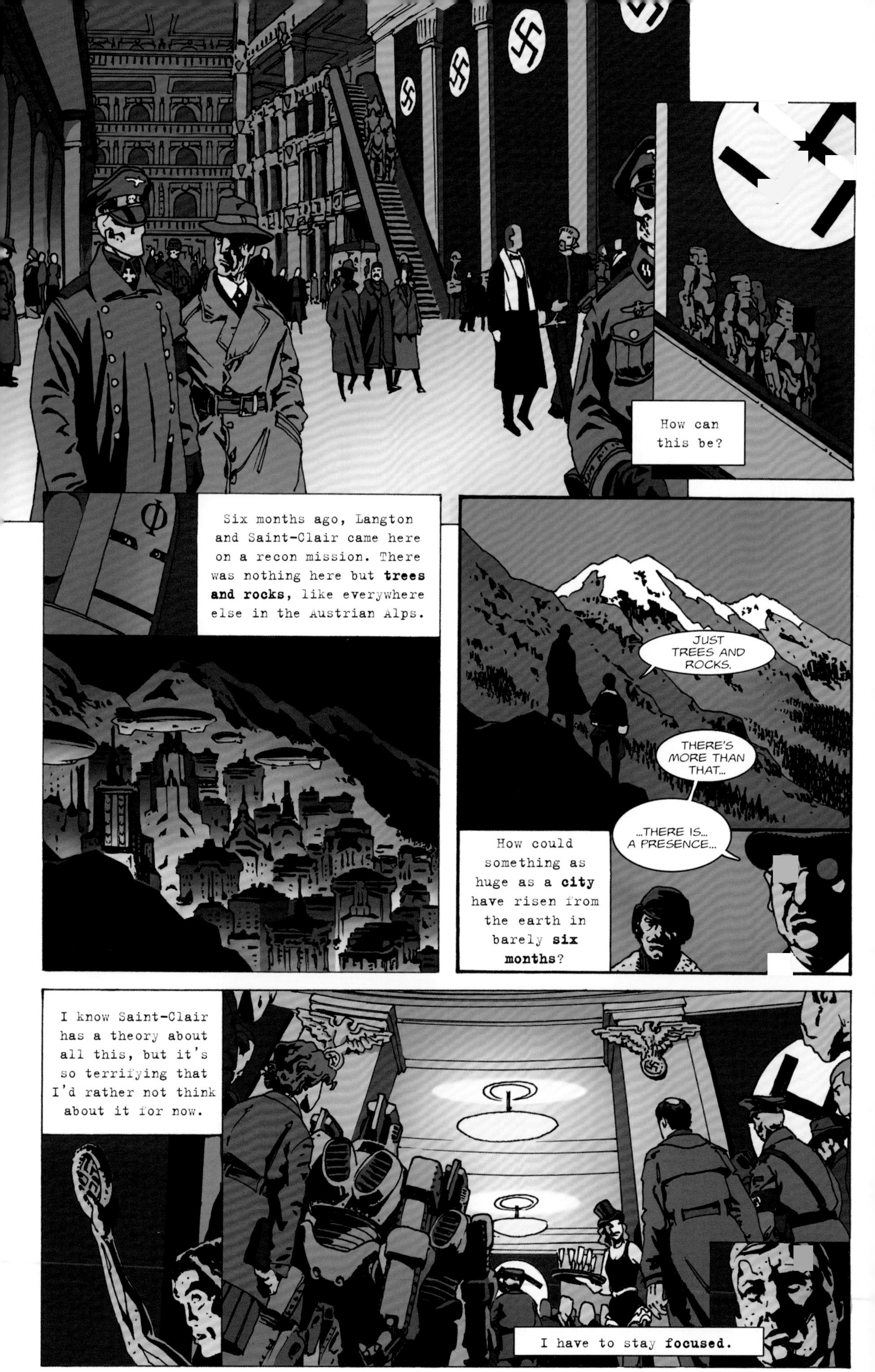
How can this be?
Six months ago, Langton and Saint-Clair came here on a recon mission. There was nothing here but **trees and rocks**, like everywhere else in the Austrian Alps.
JUST TREES AND ROCKS.
THERE'S MORE THAN THAT...
...THERE IS... A PRESENCE...
How could something as huge as a **city** have risen from the earth in barely **six months**?
I know Saint-Clair has a theory about all this, but it's so terrifying that I'd rather not think about it for now.
I have to stay **focused.**

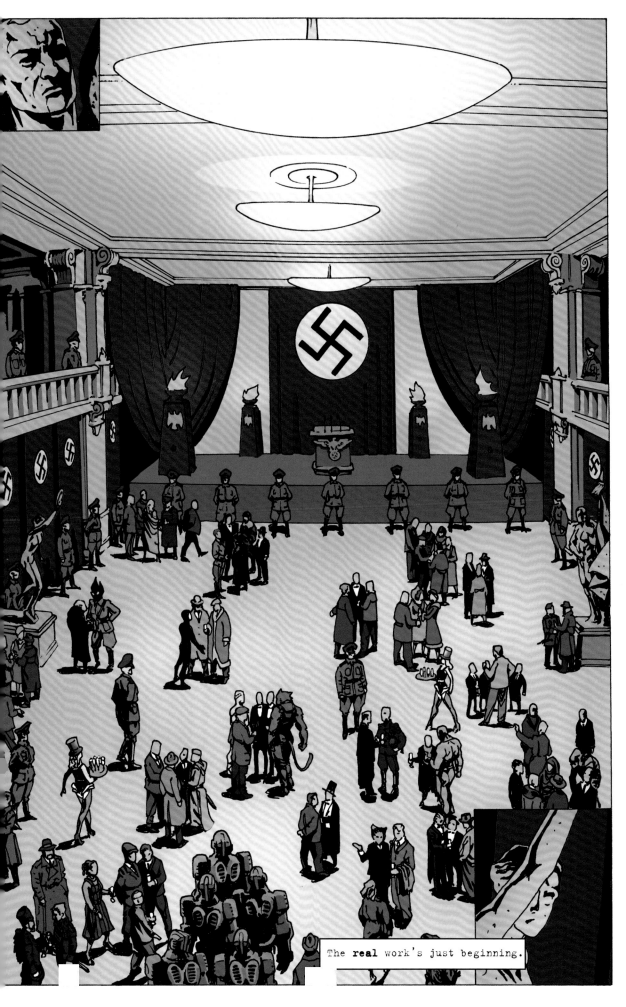

The **real** work's just beginning.

THOMAS!

HOW NICE TO SEE YOU AGAIN!

HELLO, DEAN. HOW HAVE YOU BEEN SINCE THE GORGON CASE?

...A MILITARY EXPERIMENT.

OH YES -- MOLECULAR BIPARTITION. I READ ROSNY'S BOOK ON GRANTAIGLE.

GRR...

TOO MANY TOTENKOPFS HERE!

Looks like "We"'s secret services were **right**.

BARCELONA LIES IN **RUINS**! WHAT NEXT?

I'D RATHER RAZE SPAIN **TO THE GROUND** THAN LOSE IT TO THE PARTISANS.

LET'S CHANGE THE SUBJECT, SHALL WE? YOU MIGHT BE MAKING THESE MECHANIZED BOLSHEVIKS A BIT **GLUM**.

UNLESS, OF COURSE, THEY SECRETLY **AGREE** WITH US.

Dean Dickson. Tom Terence, Tigrefax and Kun-Son, the last Atlantean.

WELL IF THAT'S THE CASE, I'M DOING THEIR DIRTY WORK FOR THEM! **HA HA!**

Gog and Falange are here as well.

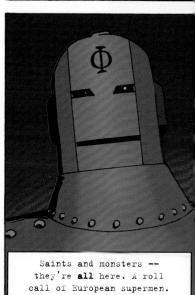

Saints and monsters -- they're **all** here. A roll call of European supermen.

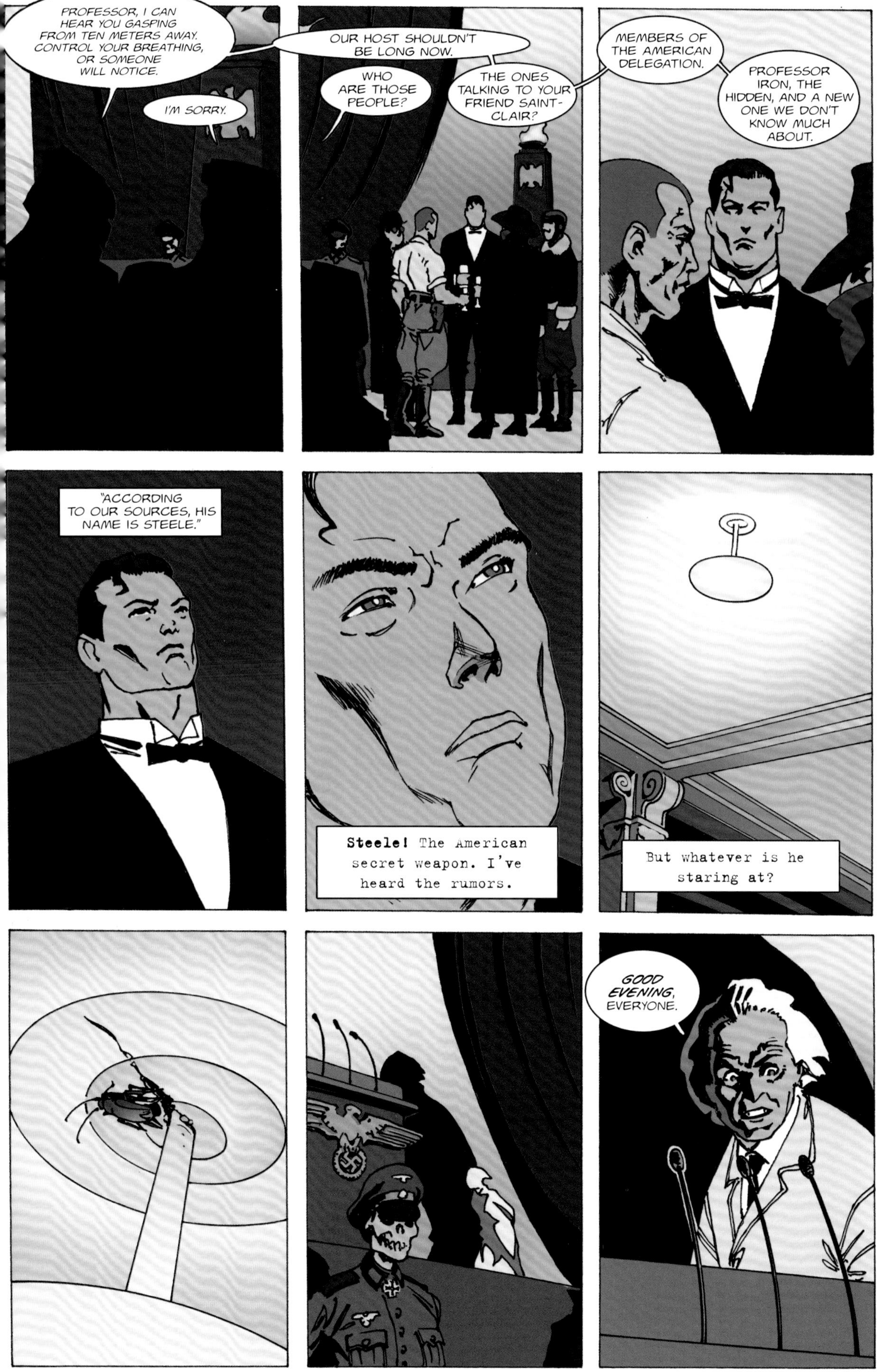
PROFESSOR, I CAN HEAR YOU GASPING FROM TEN METERS AWAY. CONTROL YOUR BREATHING, OR SOMEONE WILL NOTICE.
I'M SORRY.
OUR HOST SHOULDN'T BE LONG NOW.
WHO ARE THOSE PEOPLE?
THE ONES TALKING TO YOUR FRIEND SAINT-CLAIR?
MEMBERS OF THE AMERICAN DELEGATION.
PROFESSOR IRON, THE HIDDEN, AND A NEW ONE WE DON'T KNOW MUCH ABOUT.
"ACCORDING TO OUR SOURCES, HIS NAME IS STEELE."
Steele! The American secret weapon. I've heard the rumors.
But whatever is he staring at?
GOOD EVENING, EVERYONE.

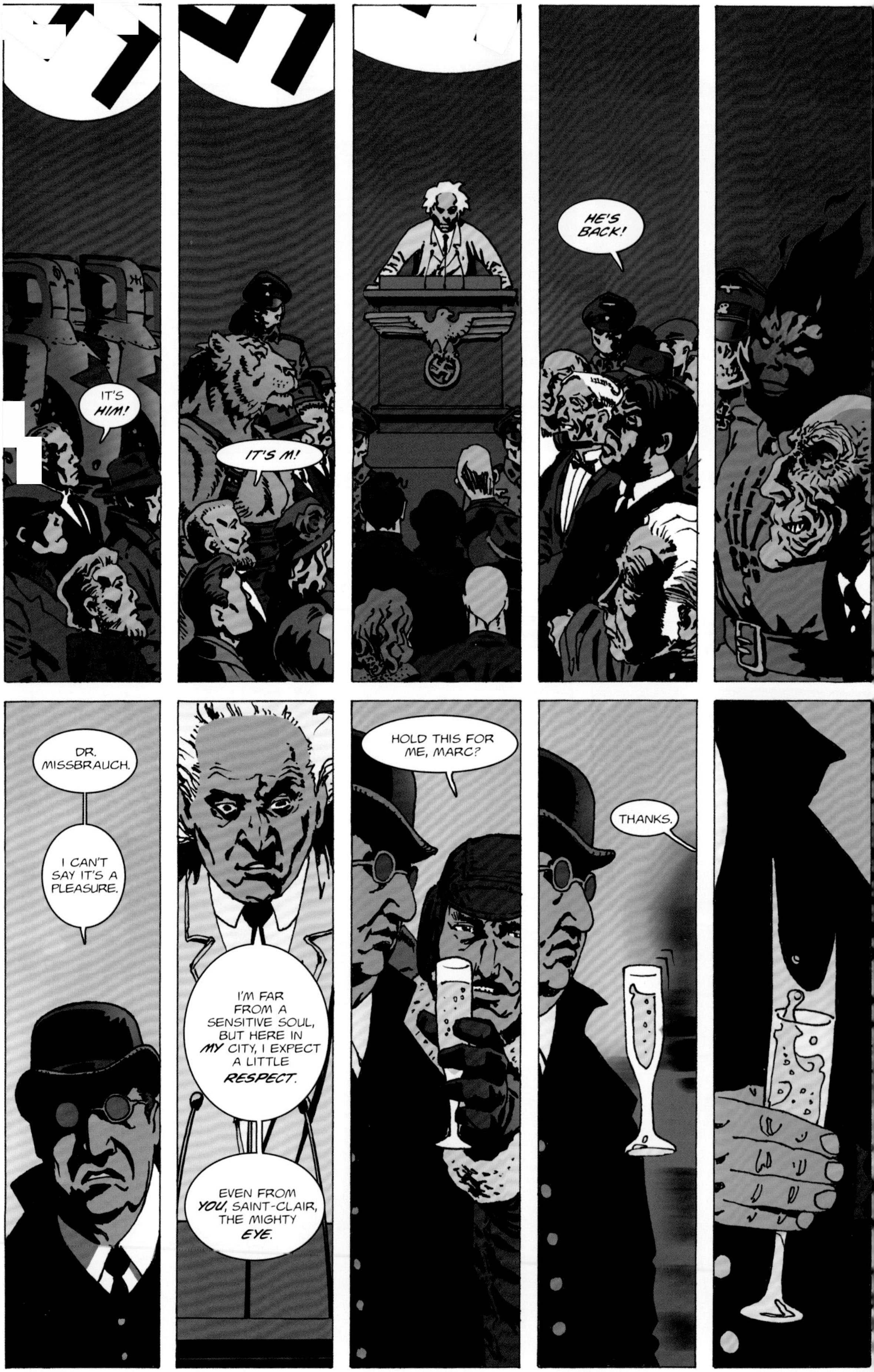
IT'S HIM!
IT'S M!
HE'S BACK!
DR. MISSBRAUCH.
I CAN'T SAY IT'S A PLEASURE.
I'M FAR FROM A SENSITIVE SOUL, BUT HERE IN MY CITY, I EXPECT A LITTLE RESPECT.
EVEN FROM YOU, SAINT-CLAIR, THE MIGHTY EYE.
HOLD THIS FOR ME, MARC?
THANKS.

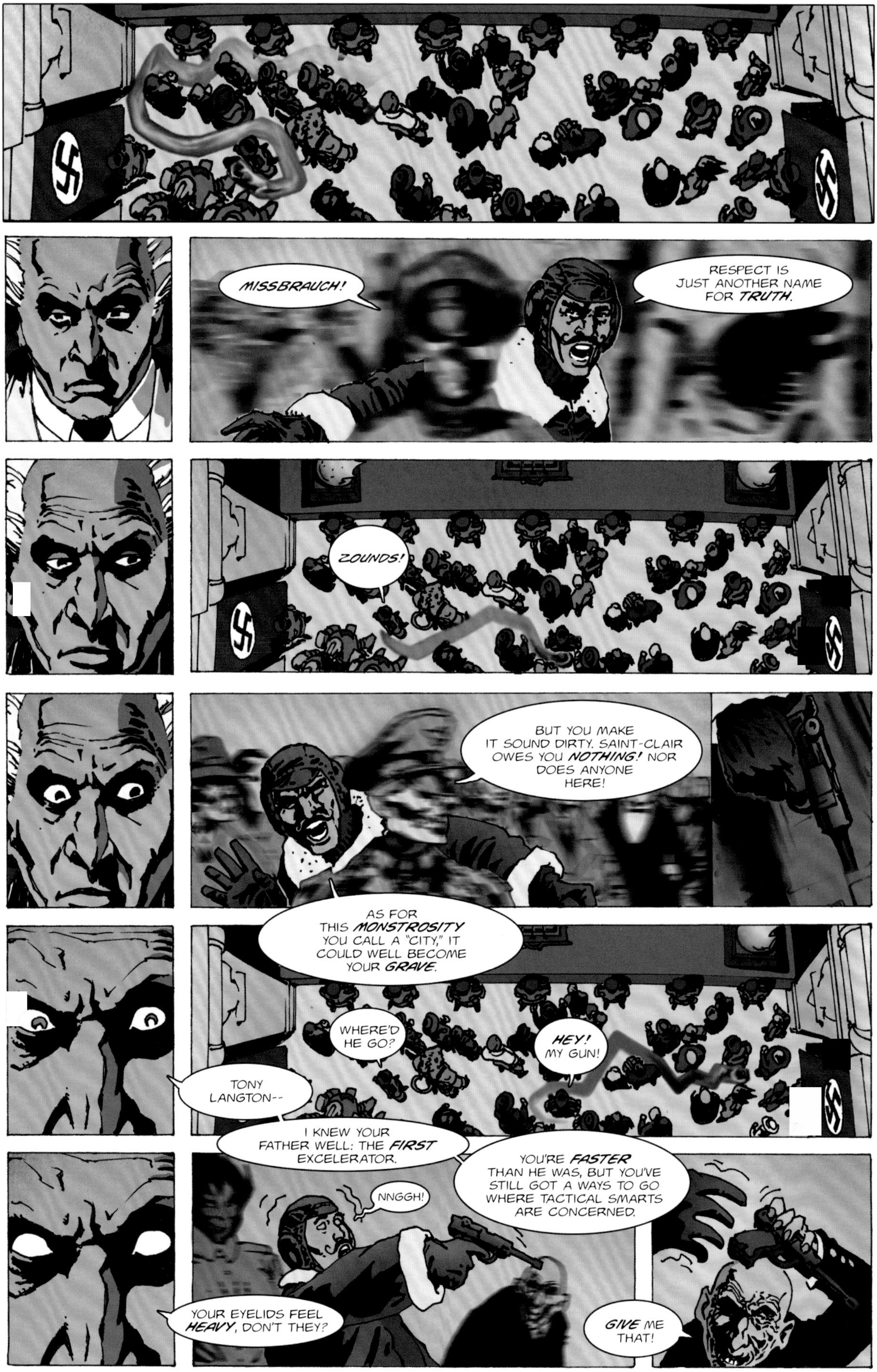

MISSBRAUCH!
RESPECT IS JUST ANOTHER NAME FOR TRUTH.
ZOUNDS!
BUT YOU MAKE IT SOUND DIRTY. SAINT-CLAIR OWES YOU NOTHING! NOR DOES ANYONE HERE!
AS FOR THIS MONSTROSITY YOU CALL A "CITY," IT COULD WELL BECOME YOUR GRAVE.
WHERE'D HE GO?
HEY! MY GUN!
TONY LANGTON--
I KNEW YOUR FATHER WELL: THE FIRST EXCELERATOR.
NNGGH!
YOU'RE FASTER THAN HE WAS, BUT YOU'VE STILL GOT A WAYS TO GO WHERE TACTICAL SMARTS ARE CONCERNED.
YOUR EYELIDS FEEL HEAVY, DON'T THEY?
GIVE ME THAT!

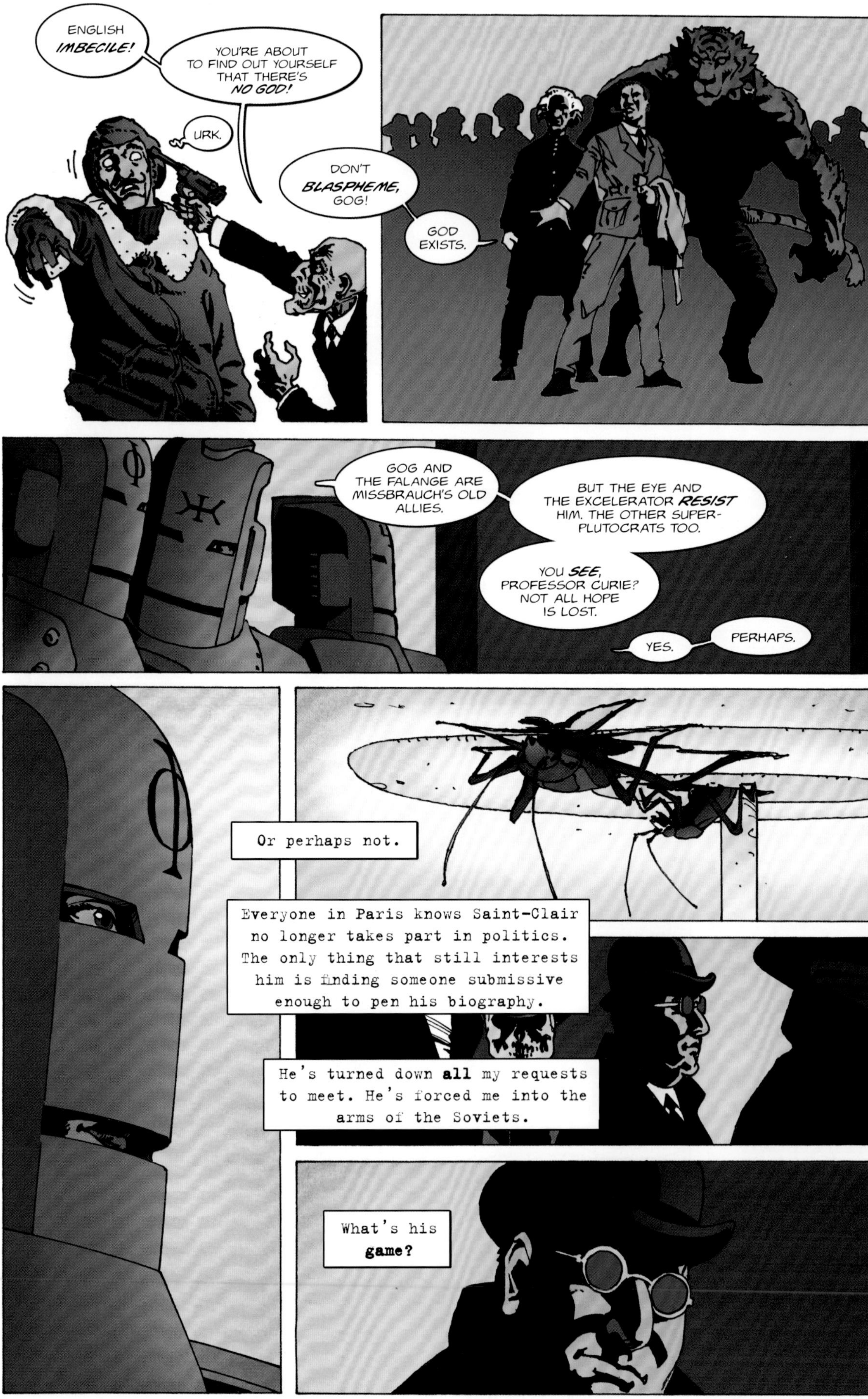
ENGLISH *IMBECILE!*
YOU'RE ABOUT TO FIND OUT YOURSELF THAT THERE'S *NO GOD!*
URK.
DON'T *BLASPHEME,* GOG!
GOD EXISTS.
GOG AND THE FALANGE ARE MISSBRAUCH'S OLD ALLIES.
BUT THE EYE AND THE EXCELERATOR *RESIST* HIM. THE OTHER SUPER-PLUTOCRATS TOO.
YOU *SEE,* PROFESSOR CURIE? NOT ALL HOPE IS LOST.
YES.
PERHAPS.
Or perhaps not.
Everyone in Paris knows Saint-Clair no longer takes part in politics. The only thing that still interests him is finding someone submissive enough to pen his biography.
He's turned down **all** my requests to meet. He's forced me into the arms of the Soviets.
What's his **game?**

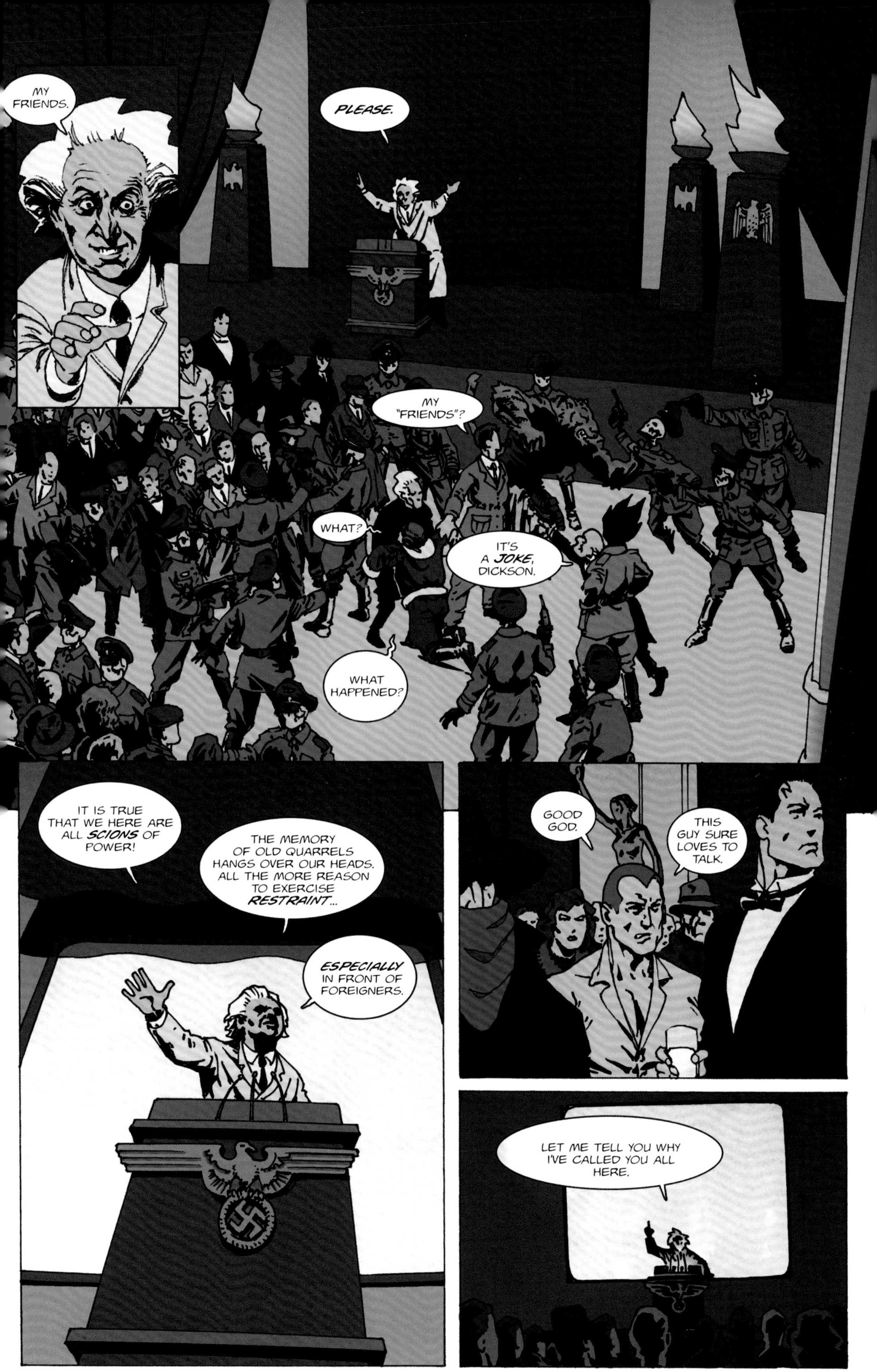
MY FRIENDS.
PLEASE.
MY "FRIENDS"?
WHAT?
IT'S A JOKE, DICKSON.
WHAT HAPPENED?
IT IS TRUE THAT WE HERE ARE ALL SCIONS OF POWER!
THE MEMORY OF OLD QUARRELS HANGS OVER OUR HEADS. ALL THE MORE REASON TO EXERCISE RESTRAINT...
ESPECIALLY IN FRONT OF FOREIGNERS.
GOOD GOD.
THIS GUY SURE LOVES TO TALK.
LET ME TELL YOU WHY I'VE CALLED YOU ALL HERE.

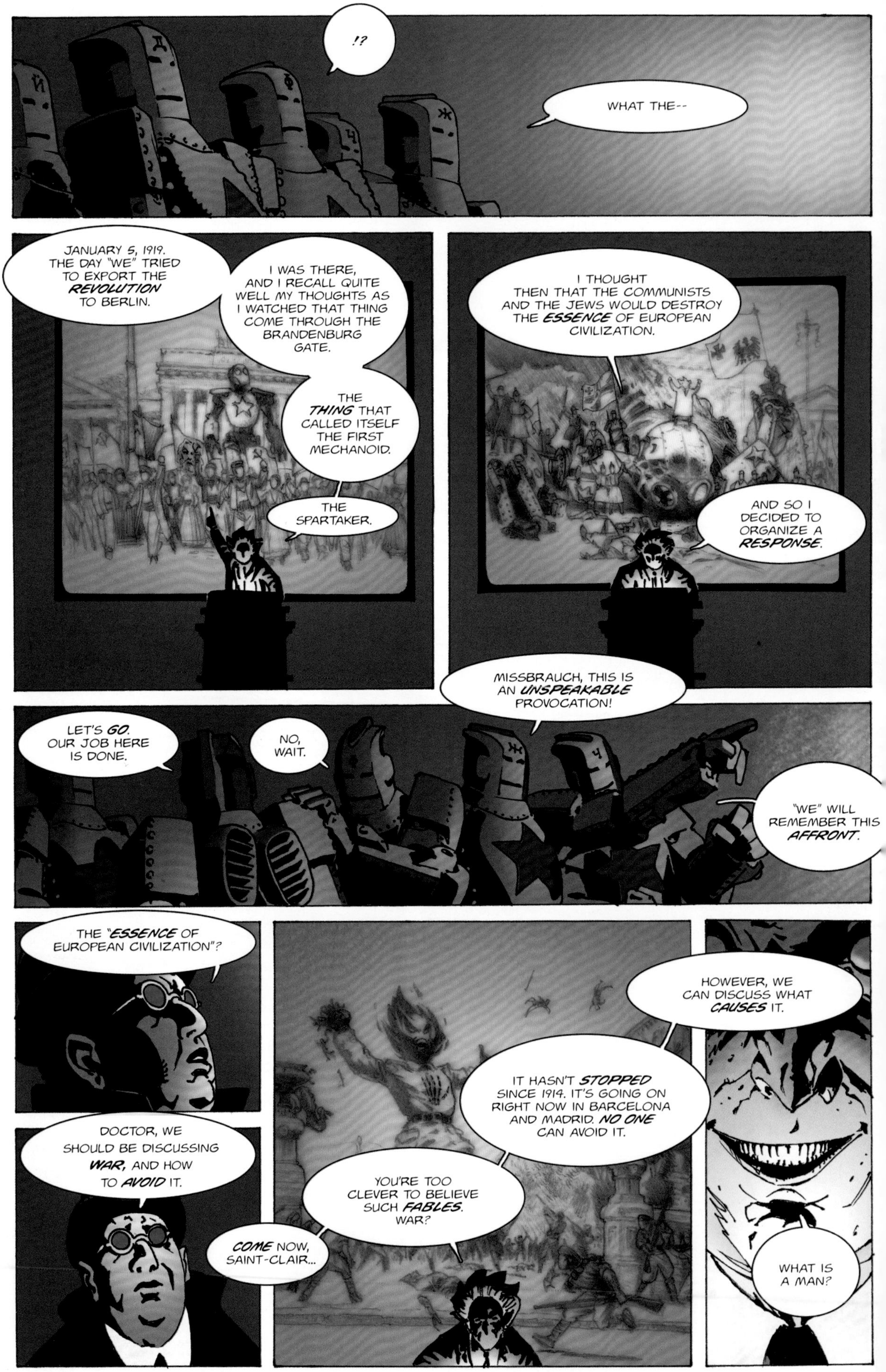
!?
WHAT THE--
JANUARY 5, 1919. THE DAY "WE" TRIED TO EXPORT THE REVOLUTION TO BERLIN.
I WAS THERE, AND I RECALL QUITE WELL MY THOUGHTS AS I WATCHED THAT THING COME THROUGH THE BRANDENBURG GATE.
THE THING THAT CALLED ITSELF THE FIRST MECHANOID.
THE SPARTAKER.
I THOUGHT THEN THAT THE COMMUNISTS AND THE JEWS WOULD DESTROY THE ESSENCE OF EUROPEAN CIVILIZATION.
AND SO I DECIDED TO ORGANIZE A RESPONSE.
LET'S GO. OUR JOB HERE IS DONE.
NO, WAIT.
MISSBRAUCH, THIS IS AN UNSPEAKABLE PROVOCATION!
"WE" WILL REMEMBER THIS AFFRONT.
THE "ESSENCE OF EUROPEAN CIVILIZATION"?
DOCTOR, WE SHOULD BE DISCUSSING WAR, AND HOW TO AVOID IT.
COME NOW, SAINT-CLAIR...
YOU'RE TOO CLEVER TO BELIEVE SUCH FABLES. WAR?
IT HASN'T STOPPED SINCE 1914. IT'S GOING ON RIGHT NOW IN BARCELONA AND MADRID. NO ONE CAN AVOID IT.
HOWEVER, WE CAN DISCUSS WHAT CAUSES IT.
WHAT IS A MAN?

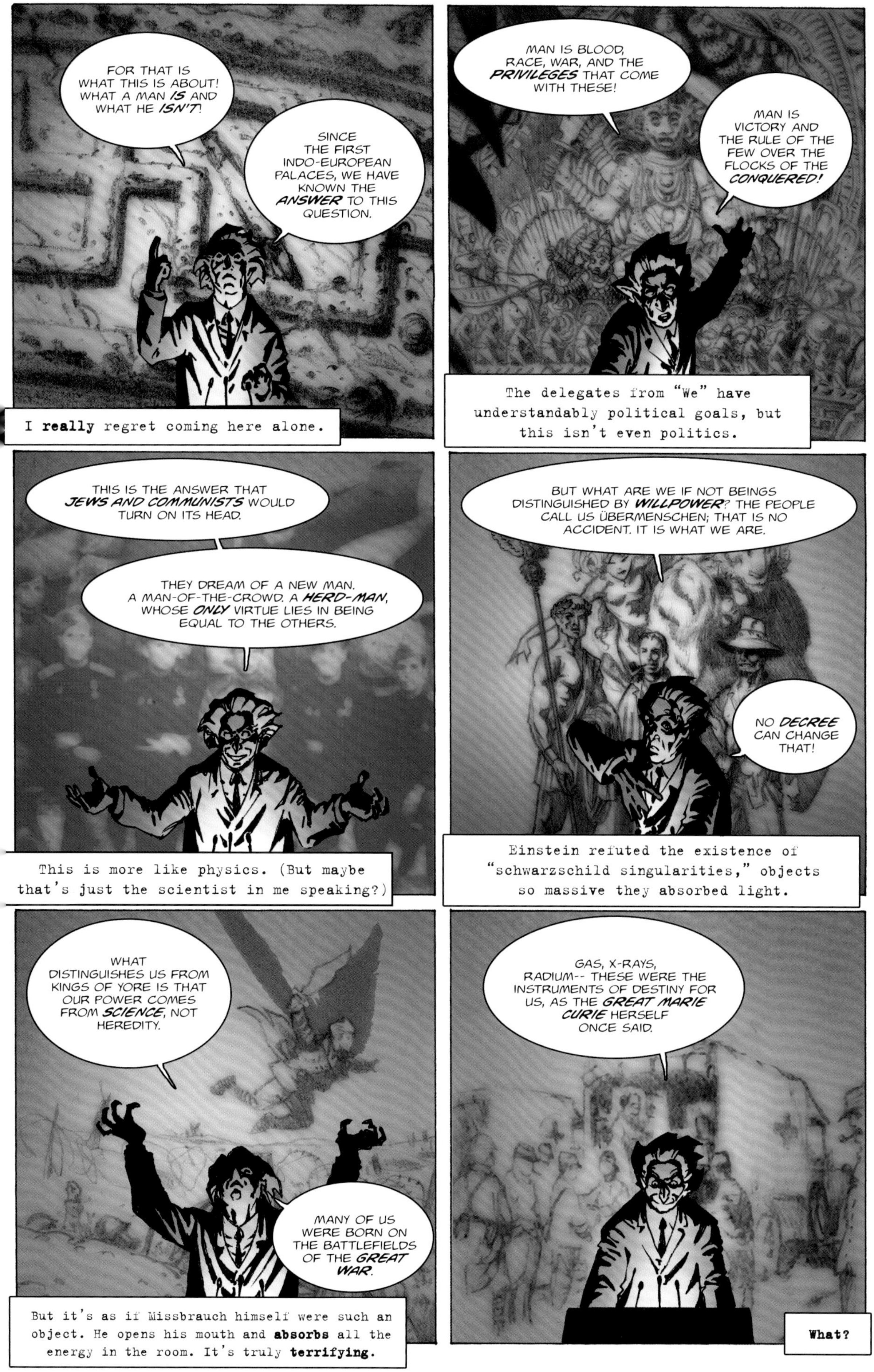
FOR THAT IS WHAT THIS IS ABOUT! WHAT A MAN IS AND WHAT HE ISN'T!
SINCE THE FIRST INDO-EUROPEAN PALACES, WE HAVE KNOWN THE ANSWER TO THIS QUESTION.
I really regret coming here alone.
MAN IS BLOOD, RACE, WAR, AND THE PRIVILEGES THAT COME WITH THESE!
MAN IS VICTORY AND THE RULE OF THE FEW OVER THE FLOCKS OF THE CONQUERED!
The delegates from "We" have understandably political goals, but this isn't even politics.
THIS IS THE ANSWER THAT JEWS AND COMMUNISTS WOULD TURN ON ITS HEAD.
THEY DREAM OF A NEW MAN. A MAN-OF-THE-CROWD. A HERD-MAN, WHOSE ONLY VIRTUE LIES IN BEING EQUAL TO THE OTHERS.
This is more like physics. (But maybe that's just the scientist in me speaking?)
BUT WHAT ARE WE IF NOT BEINGS DISTINGUISHED BY WILLPOWER? THE PEOPLE CALL US ÜBERMENSCHEN; THAT IS NO ACCIDENT. IT IS WHAT WE ARE.
NO DECREE CAN CHANGE THAT!
Einstein refuted the existence of "schwarzschild singularities," objects so massive they absorbed light.
WHAT DISTINGUISHES US FROM KINGS OF YORE IS THAT OUR POWER COMES FROM SCIENCE, NOT HEREDITY.
MANY OF US WERE BORN ON THE BATTLEFIELDS OF THE GREAT WAR.
But it's as if Missbrauch himself were such an object. He opens his mouth and absorbs all the energy in the room. It's truly terrifying.
GAS, X-RAYS, RADIUM-- THESE WERE THE INSTRUMENTS OF DESTINY FOR US, AS THE GREAT MARIE CURIE HERSELF ONCE SAID.
What?

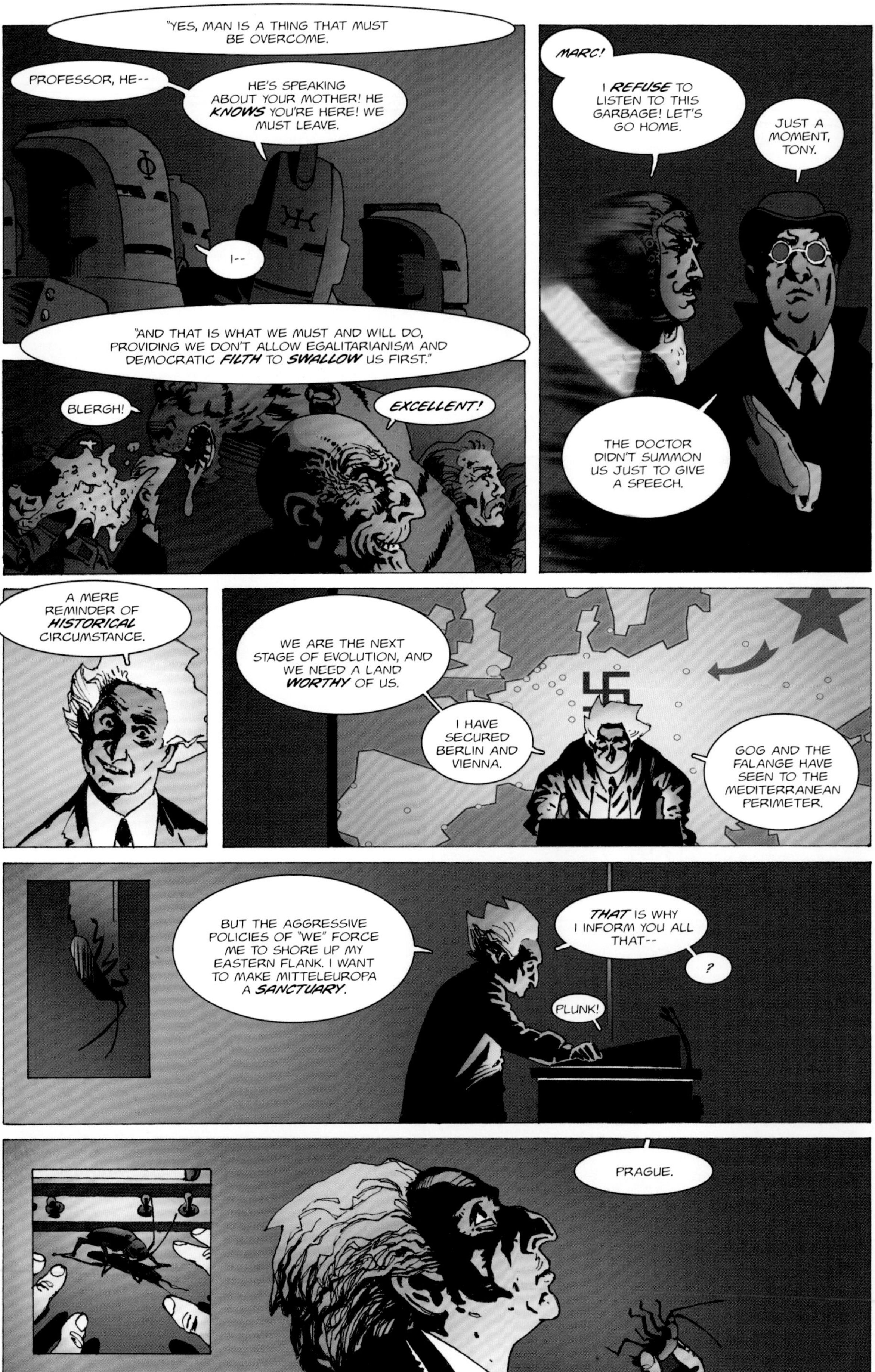
"YES, MAN IS A THING THAT MUST BE OVERCOME.
PROFESSOR, HE--
HE'S SPEAKING ABOUT YOUR MOTHER! HE KNOWS YOU'RE HERE! WE MUST LEAVE.
I--
"AND THAT IS WHAT WE MUST AND WILL DO, PROVIDING WE DON'T ALLOW EGALITARIANISM AND DEMOCRATIC FILTH TO SWALLOW US FIRST."
BLERGH!
EXCELLENT!
MARC!
I REFUSE TO LISTEN TO THIS GARBAGE! LET'S GO HOME.
JUST A MOMENT, TONY.
THE DOCTOR DIDN'T SUMMON US JUST TO GIVE A SPEECH.
A MERE REMINDER OF HISTORICAL CIRCUMSTANCE.
WE ARE THE NEXT STAGE OF EVOLUTION, AND WE NEED A LAND WORTHY OF US.
I HAVE SECURED BERLIN AND VIENNA.
GOG AND THE FALANGE HAVE SEEN TO THE MEDITERRANEAN PERIMETER.
BUT THE AGGRESSIVE POLICIES OF "WE" FORCE ME TO SHORE UP MY EASTERN FLANK. I WANT TO MAKE MITTELEUROPA A SANCTUARY.
THAT IS WHY I INFORM YOU ALL THAT--
?
PLUNK!
PRAGUE.

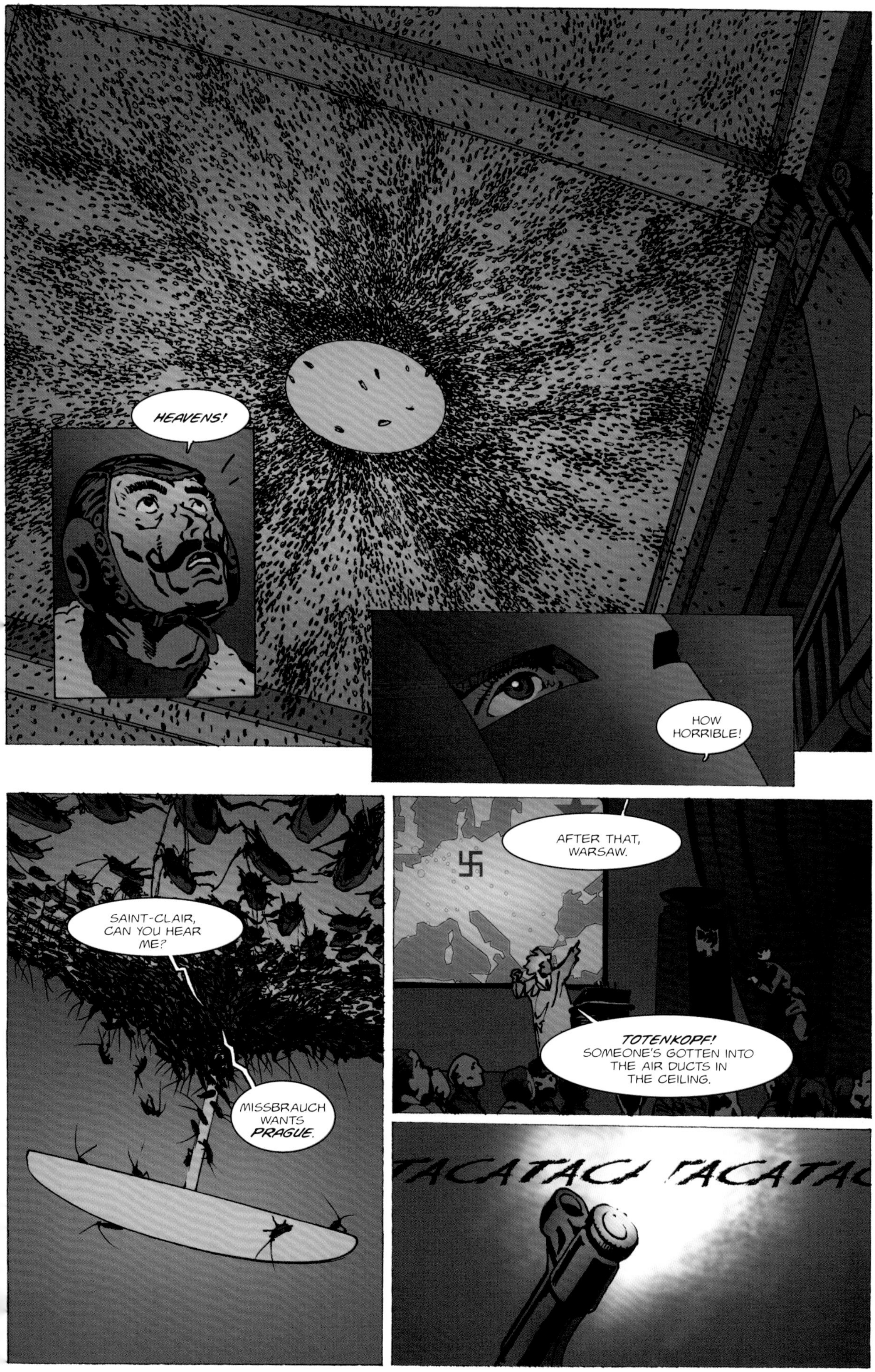
HEAVENS!
HOW HORRIBLE!
SAINT-CLAIR, CAN YOU HEAR ME?
MISSBRAUCH WANTS PRAGUE.
AFTER THAT, WARSAW.
TOTENKOPF! SOMEONE'S GOTTEN INTO THE AIR DUCTS IN THE CEILING.
TACATAC TACATAC

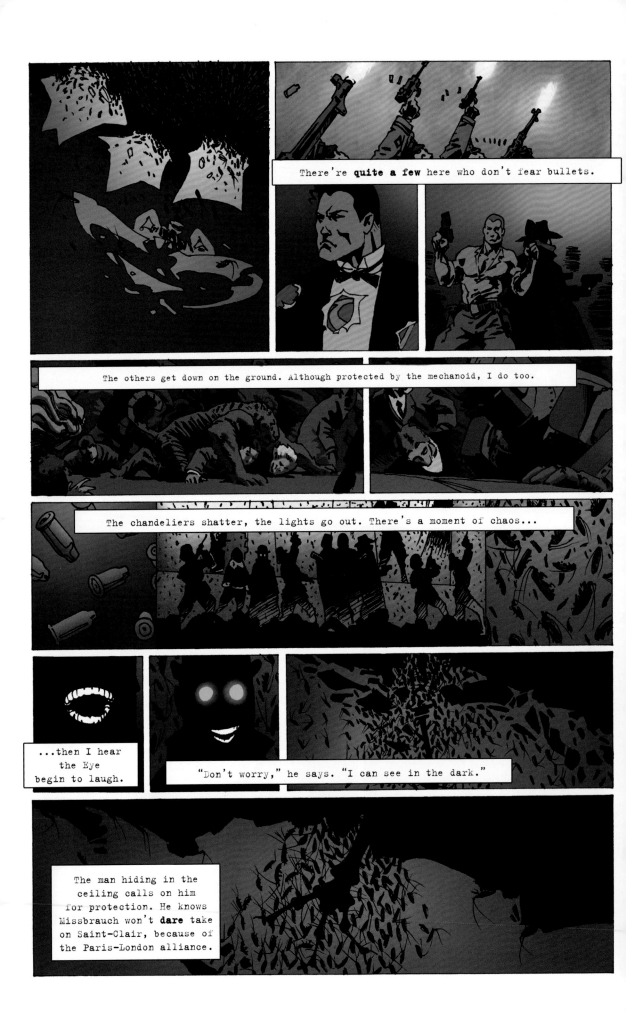

There're **quite a few** here who don't fear bullets.

The others get down on the ground. Although protected by the mechanoid, I do too.

The chandeliers shatter, the lights go out. There's a moment of chaos...

...then I hear the Eye begin to laugh.

"Don't worry," he says. "I can see in the dark."

The man hiding in the ceiling calls on him for protection. He knows Missbrauch won't **dare** take on Saint-Clair, because of the Paris-London alliance.

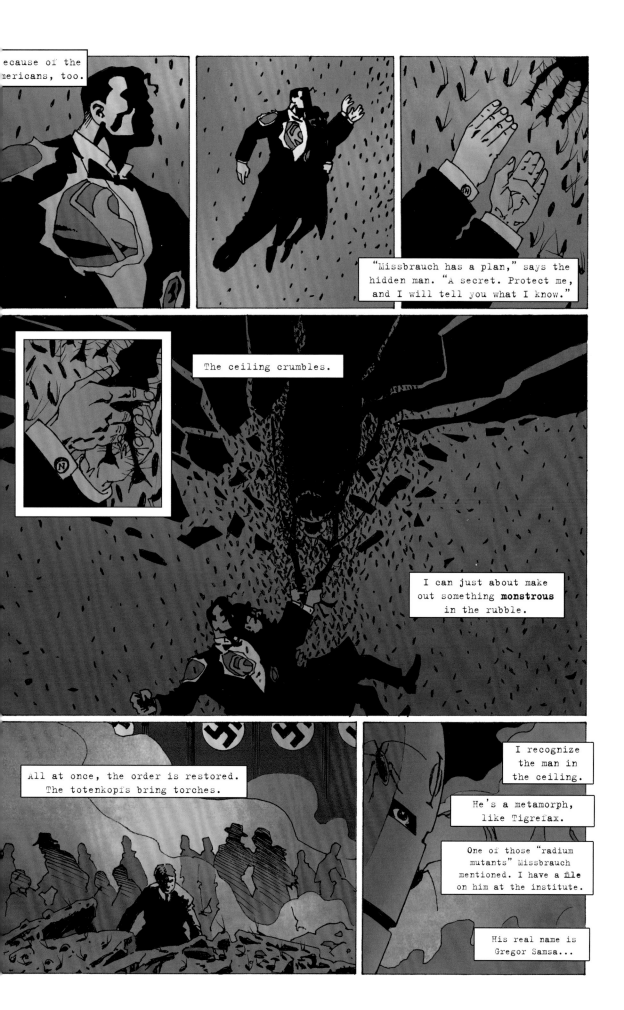

ecause of the
mericans, too.

"Missbrauch has a plan," says the
hidden man. "A secret. Protect me,
and I will tell you what I know."

The ceiling crumbles.

I can just about make
out something **monstrous**
in the rubble.

All at once, the order is restored.
The totenkopfs bring torches.

I recognize
the man in
the ceiling.

He's a metamorph,
like Tigrefax.

One of those "radium
mutants" Missbrauch
mentioned. I have a file
on him at the institute.

His real name is
Gregor Samsa...

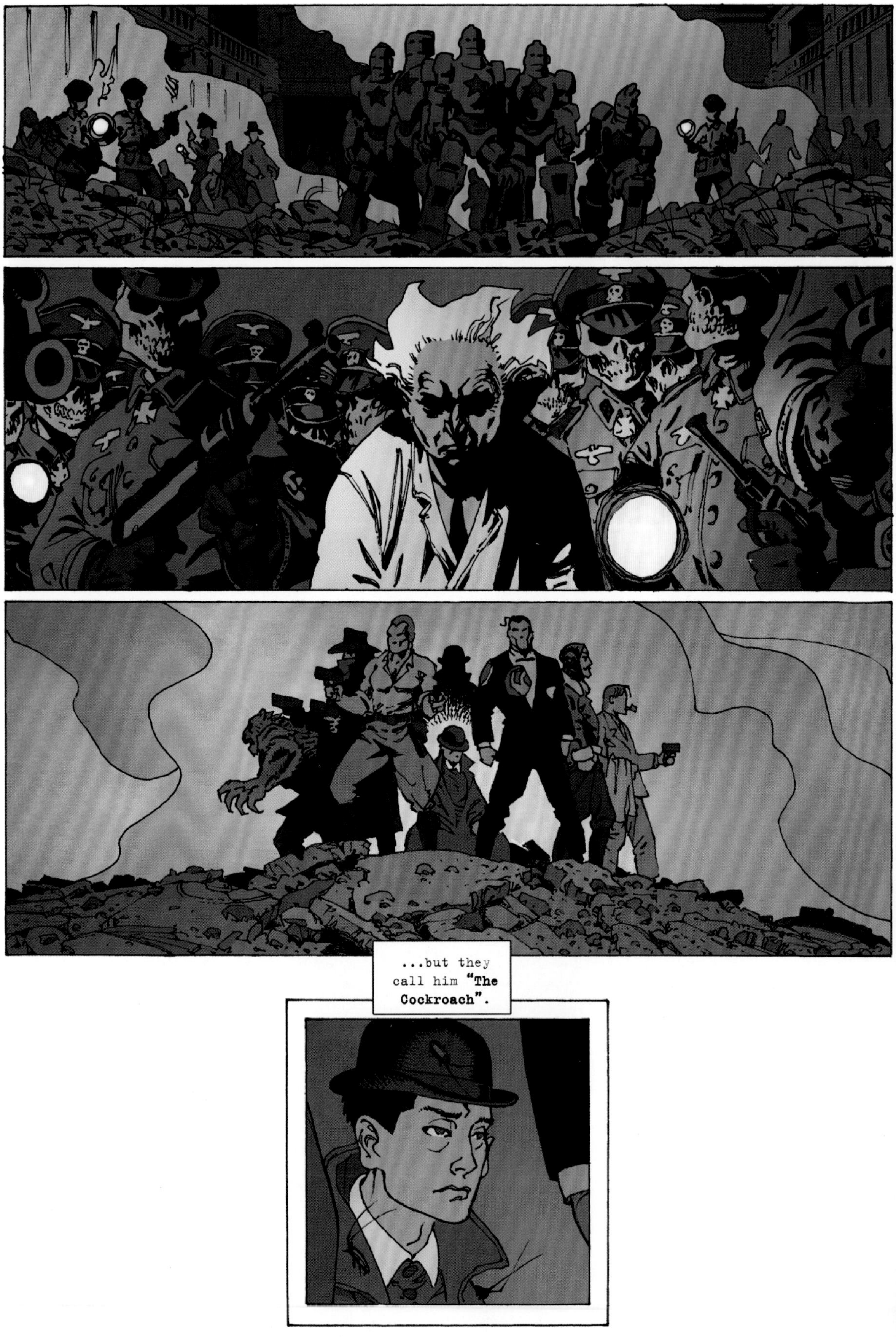
...but they call him "The Cockroach".

THE CHIMERA BRIGADE

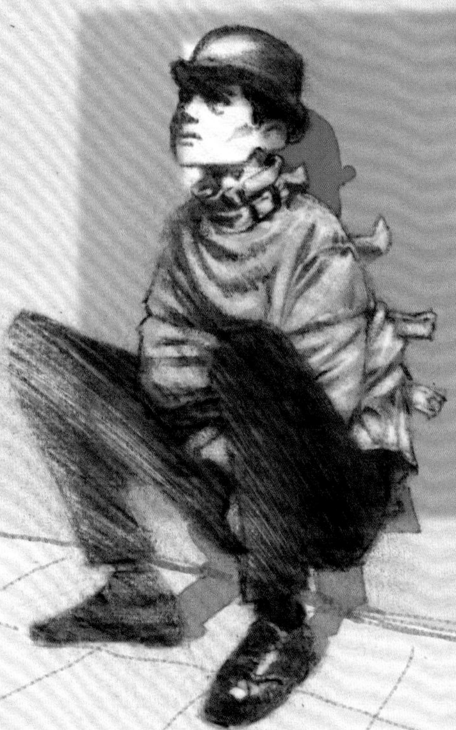

1/10

THE FINAL MISSION OF THE MAN WHO WALKS THROUGH WALLS

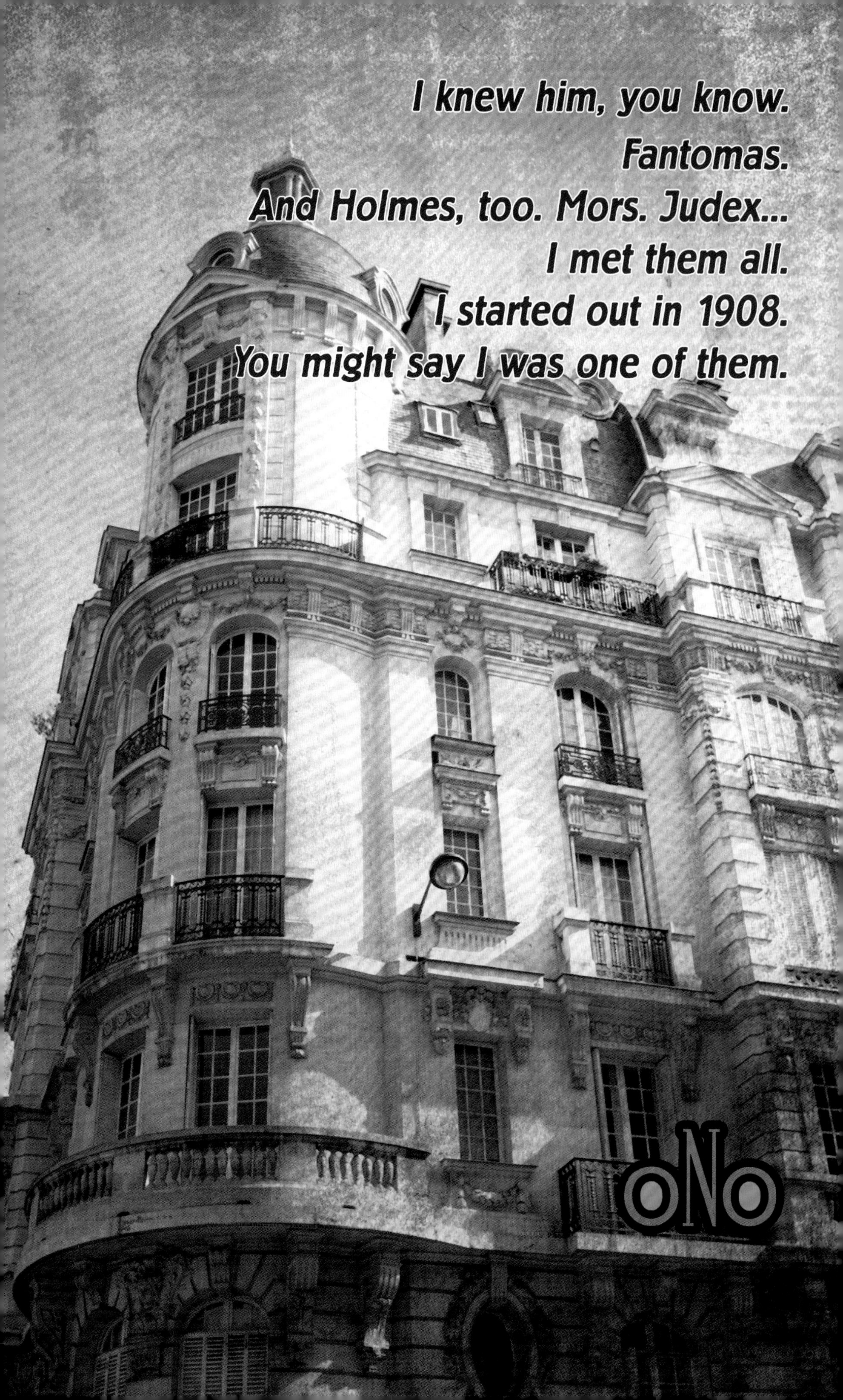
I knew him, you know.
Fantomas.
And Holmes, too. Mors. Judex...
I met them all.
I started out in 1908.
You might say I was one of them.
oNo

PARIS.
MARCH 16, 1939.

THE RADIUM INSTITUTE.

NE NOBEL PRIZE OF SHAME!

BOLSHEVIKS GO HOME!

RADIUM IS POISO

DOWN WITH THE *POISONERS!*

'SCUSE ME.

'SCUSE ME.

DOWN WITH RADIUM MONSTERS!

'SCUSE ME.

HEY! WHAT'S YOUR HURRY?

THE NOBEL PRIZE OF SHAME!

RADIUM IS POISON!

GO BACK TO MOSCOW!

STOP

DID YOU *SEE* THAT?

KIDS THESE DAYS!

GET AWAY FROM THERE, KID. IT'S BAD FOR YOUR HEALTH.

WHAT IS IT?

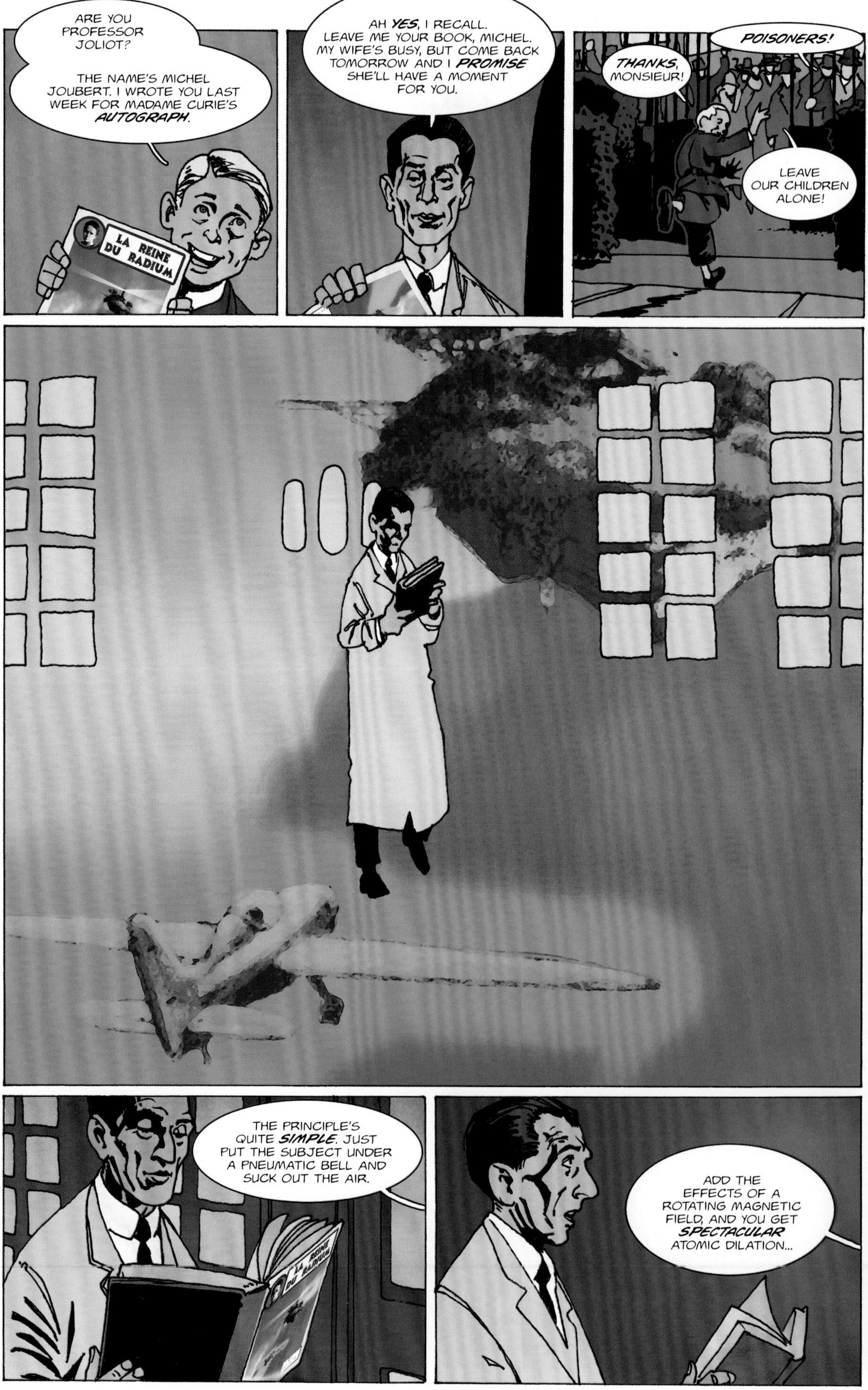
ARE YOU PROFESSOR JOLIOT?
THE NAME'S MICHEL JOUBERT. I WROTE YOU LAST WEEK FOR MADAME CURIE'S *AUTOGRAPH*.
LA REINE DU RADIUM
AH *YES*, I RECALL. LEAVE ME YOUR BOOK, MICHEL. MY WIFE'S BUSY, BUT COME BACK TOMORROW AND I *PROMISE* SHE'LL HAVE A MOMENT FOR YOU.
POISONERS!
THANKS, MONSIEUR!
LEAVE OUR CHILDREN ALONE!
THE PRINCIPLE'S QUITE *SIMPLE*. JUST PUT THE SUBJECT UNDER A PNEUMATIC BELL AND SUCK OUT THE AIR.
LA REINE DU RADIUM
ADD THE EFFECTS OF A ROTATING MAGNETIC FIELD, AND YOU GET *SPECTACULAR* ATOMIC DILATION...

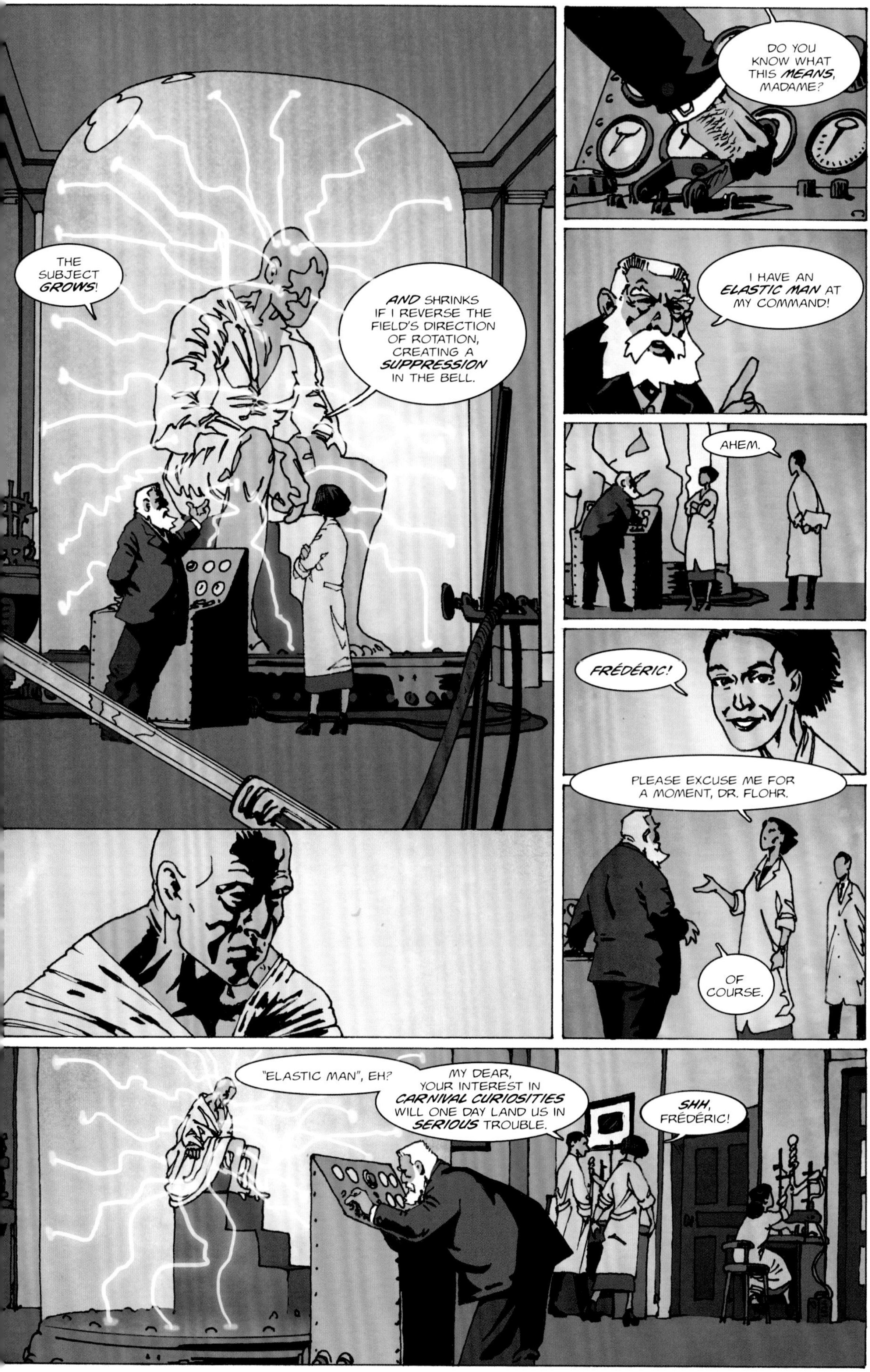
THE SUBJECT GROWS!
AND SHRINKS IF I REVERSE THE FIELD'S DIRECTION OF ROTATION, CREATING A SUPPRESSION IN THE BELL.
DO YOU KNOW WHAT THIS MEANS, MADAME?
I HAVE AN ELASTIC MAN AT MY COMMAND!
AHEM.
FRÉDÉRIC!
PLEASE EXCUSE ME FOR A MOMENT, DR. FLOHR.
OF COURSE.
"ELASTIC MAN", EH?
MY DEAR, YOUR INTEREST IN CARNIVAL CURIOSITIES WILL ONE DAY LAND US IN SERIOUS TROUBLE.
SHH, FRÉDÉRIC!

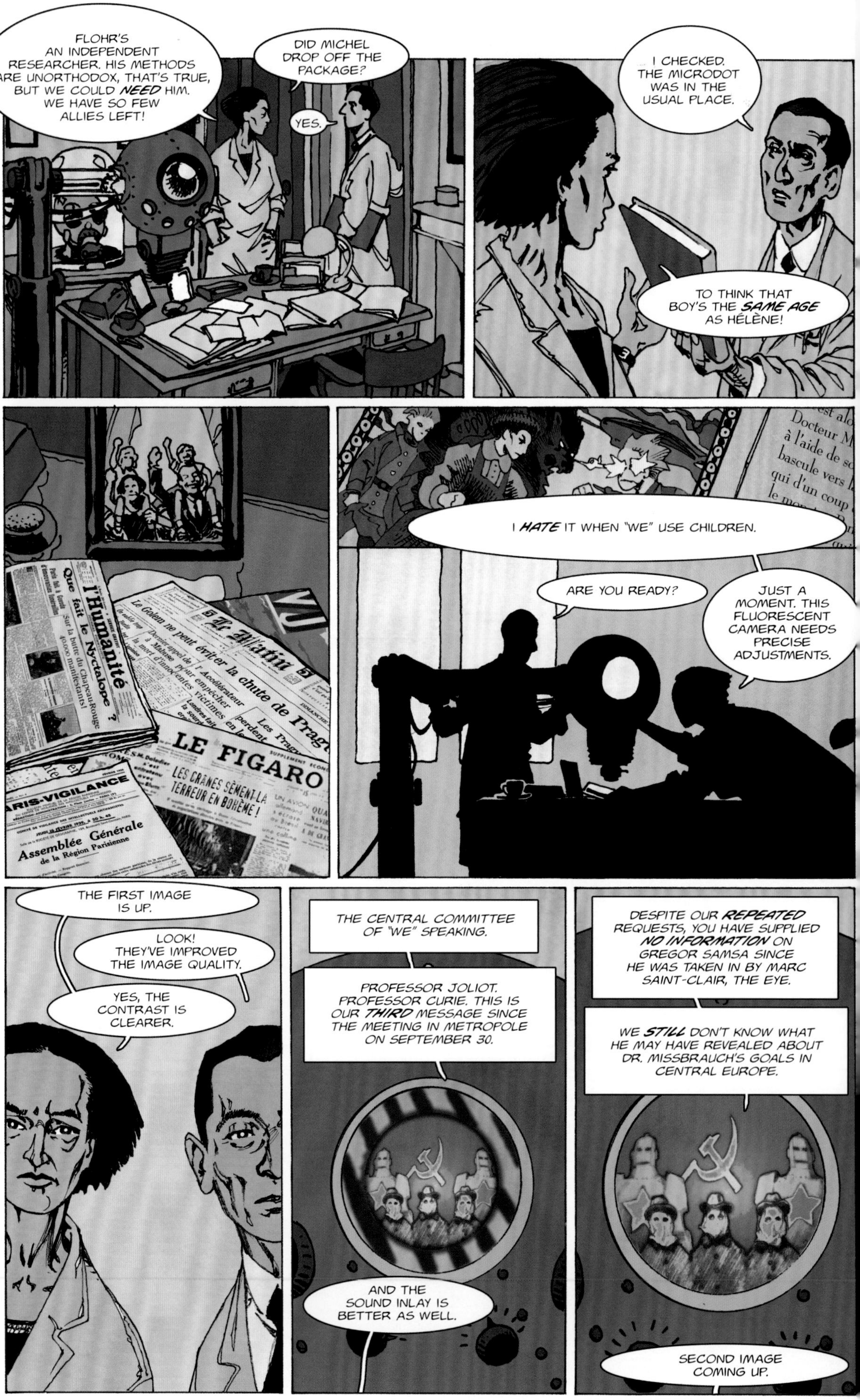

FLOHR'S AN INDEPENDENT RESEARCHER. HIS METHODS ARE UNORTHODOX, THAT'S TRUE, BUT WE COULD *NEED* HIM. WE HAVE SO FEW ALLIES LEFT!
DID MICHEL DROP OFF THE PACKAGE?
YES.
... I CHECKED. THE MICRODOT WAS IN THE USUAL PLACE.
TO THINK THAT BOY'S THE *SAME AGE* AS HÉLÈNE!
l'Humanité
Que fait le Nyctalope ?
Le Golem ne peut éviter la chute de Prague
LE FIGARO
LES CRANES SÈMENT LA TERREUR EN BOHÊME !
Assemblée Générale de la Région Parisienne
I *HATE* IT WHEN "WE" USE CHILDREN.
ARE YOU READY?
JUST A MOMENT. THIS FLUORESCENT CAMERA NEEDS PRECISE ADJUSTMENTS.
THE FIRST IMAGE IS UP.
LOOK! THEY'VE IMPROVED THE IMAGE QUALITY.
YES, THE CONTRAST IS CLEARER.
THE CENTRAL COMMITTEE OF "WE" SPEAKING.
PROFESSOR JOLIOT. PROFESSOR CURIE. THIS IS OUR *THIRD* MESSAGE SINCE THE MEETING IN METROPOLE ON SEPTEMBER 30.
AND THE SOUND INLAY IS BETTER AS WELL.
DESPITE OUR *REPEATED* REQUESTS, YOU HAVE SUPPLIED *NO INFORMATION* ON GREGOR SAMSA SINCE HE WAS TAKEN IN BY MARC SAINT-CLAIR, THE EYE.
WE *STILL* DON'T KNOW WHAT HE MAY HAVE REVEALED ABOUT DR. MISSBRAUCH'S GOALS IN CENTRAL EUROPE.
SECOND IMAGE COMING UP.

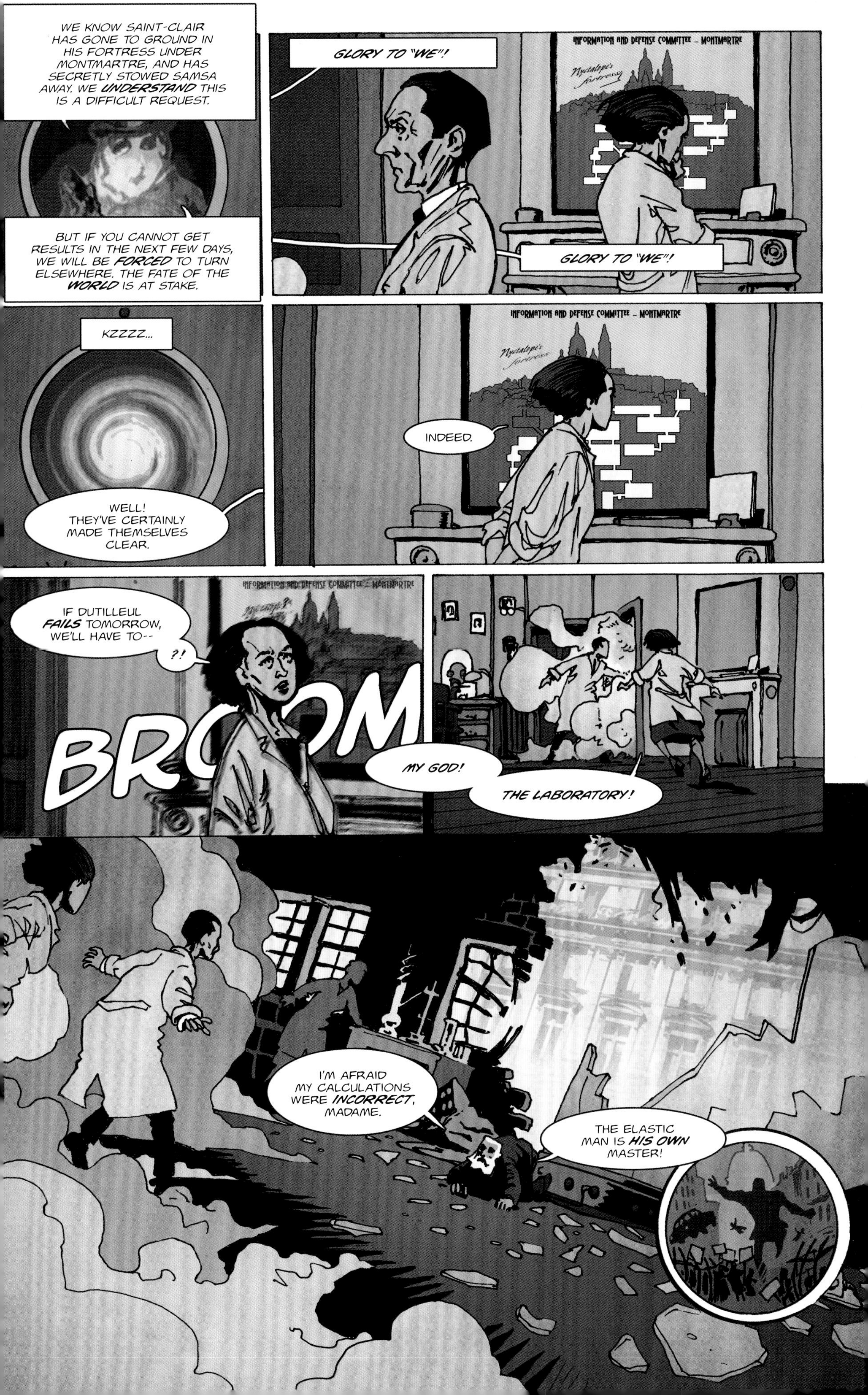
WE KNOW SAINT-CLAIR HAS GONE TO GROUND IN HIS FORTRESS UNDER MONTMARTRE, AND HAS SECRETLY STOWED SAMSA AWAY. WE UNDERSTAND THIS IS A DIFFICULT REQUEST.
BUT IF YOU CANNOT GET RESULTS IN THE NEXT FEW DAYS, WE WILL BE FORCED TO TURN ELSEWHERE. THE FATE OF THE WORLD IS AT STAKE.
GLORY TO "WE"!
INFORMATION AND DEFENSE COMMITTEE – MONTMARTRE
Nyctalope's fortress
GLORY TO "WE"!
KZZZZ...
WELL! THEY'VE CERTAINLY MADE THEMSELVES CLEAR.
INFORMATION AND DEFENSE COMMITTEE – MONTMARTRE
Nyctalope's fortress
INDEED.
IF DUTILLEUL FAILS TOMORROW, WE'LL HAVE TO--
?!
BROOM
MY GOD!
THE LABORATORY!
I'M AFRAID MY CALCULATIONS WERE INCORRECT, MADAME.
THE ELASTIC MAN IS HIS OWN MASTER!

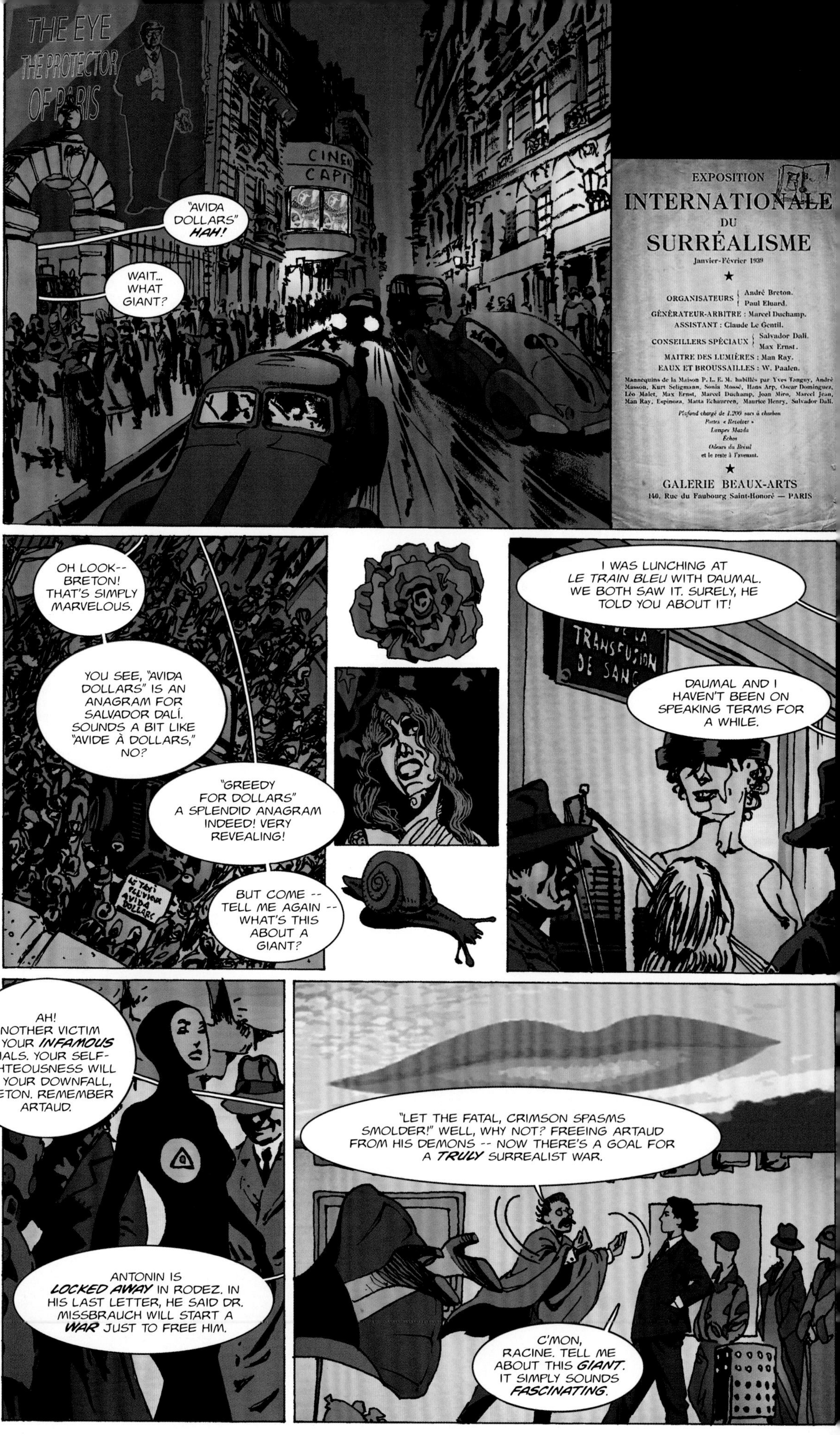
THE EYE
THE PROTECTOR
OF PARIS
CINE CAPIT
"AVIDA DOLLARS" HAH!
WAIT... WHAT GIANT?
EXPOSITION
INTERNATIONALE
DU
SURRÉALISME
Janvier-Février 1939
ORGANISATEURS André Breton. Paul Eluard.
GÉNÉRATEUR-ARBITRE : Marcel Duchamp.
ASSISTANT : Claude Le Gentil.
CONSEILLERS SPÉCIAUX Salvador Dali. Max Ernst.
MAITRE DES LUMIÈRES : Man Ray.
EAUX ET BROUSSAILLES : W. Paalen.
Mannequins de la Maison P. L. E. M. habillés par Yves Tanguy, André Masson, Kurt Seligmann, Sonia Mossé, Hans Arp, Oscar Dominguez, Léo Malet, Max Ernst, Marcel Duchamp, Joan Miro, Marcel Jean, Man Ray, Espinoza, Matta Echaurren, Maurice Henry, Salvador Dali.
Plafond chargé de 1.200 sacs à charbon
Portes « Revolver »
Lampes Mazda
Échos
Odeurs du Brésil
et le reste à l'avenant.
GALERIE BEAUX-ARTS
140, Rue du Faubourg Saint-Honoré — PARIS
OH LOOK-- BRETON! THAT'S SIMPLY MARVELOUS.
YOU SEE, "AVIDA DOLLARS" IS AN ANAGRAM FOR SALVADOR DALÍ. SOUNDS A BIT LIKE "AVIDE À DOLLARS," NO?
"GREEDY FOR DOLLARS" A SPLENDID ANAGRAM INDEED! VERY REVEALING!
BUT COME -- TELL ME AGAIN -- WHAT'S THIS ABOUT A GIANT?
AVIDA DOLLARS
I WAS LUNCHING AT LE TRAIN BLEU WITH DAUMAL. WE BOTH SAW IT. SURELY, HE TOLD YOU ABOUT IT!
TRANSFUSION DE SANG
DAUMAL AND I HAVEN'T BEEN ON SPEAKING TERMS FOR A WHILE.
AH! ANOTHER VICTIM OF YOUR INFAMOUS TRIALS. YOUR SELF-RIGHTEOUSNESS WILL BE YOUR DOWNFALL, BRETON. REMEMBER ARTAUD.
ANTONIN IS LOCKED AWAY IN RODEZ. IN HIS LAST LETTER, HE SAID DR. MISSBRAUCH WILL START A WAR JUST TO FREE HIM.
"LET THE FATAL, CRIMSON SPASMS SMOLDER!" WELL, WHY NOT? FREEING ARTAUD FROM HIS DEMONS -- NOW THERE'S A GOAL FOR A TRULY SURREALIST WAR.
C'MON, RACINE. TELL ME ABOUT THIS GIANT. IT SIMPLY SOUNDS FASCINATING.

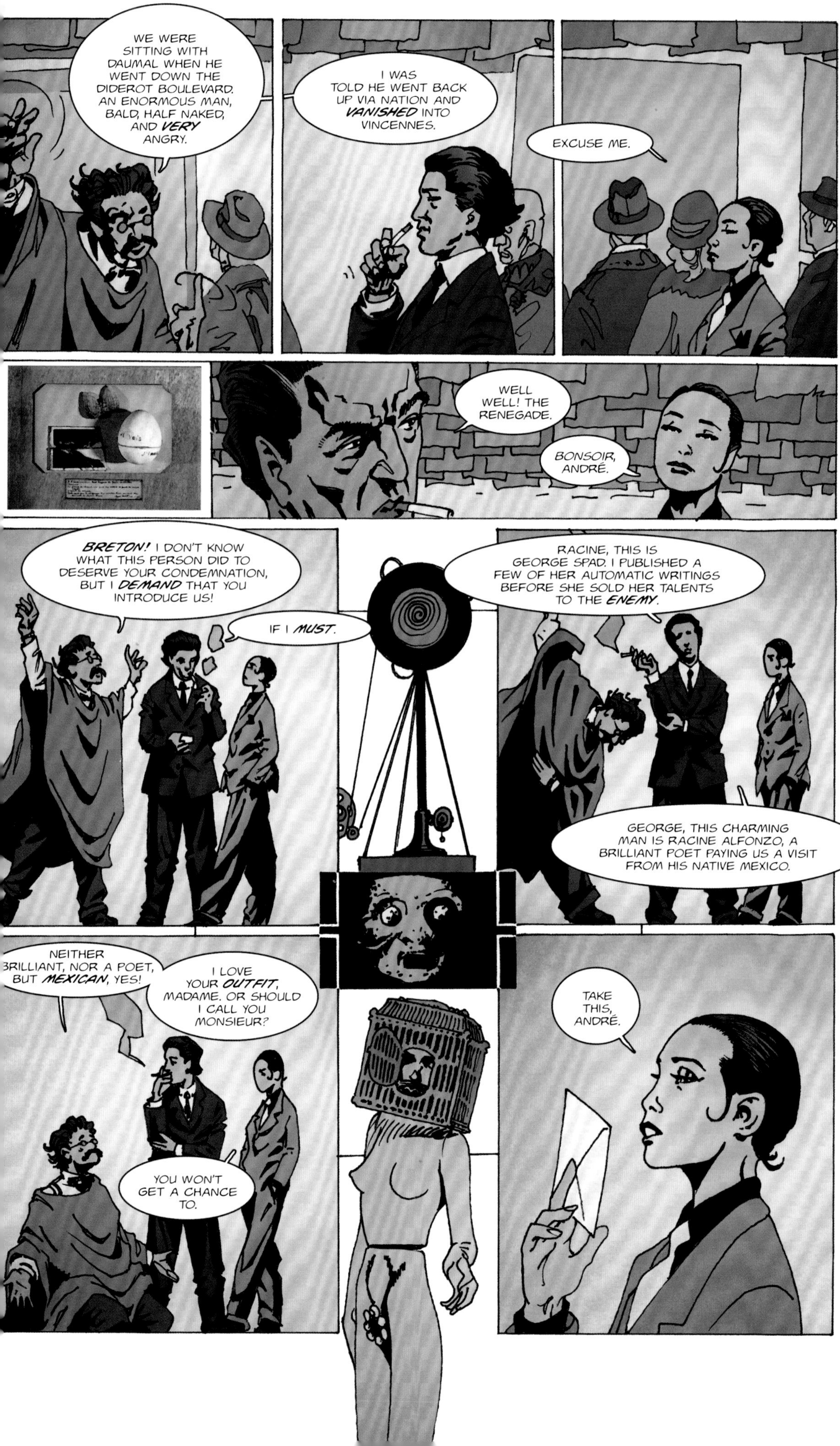
WE WERE SITTING WITH DAUMAL WHEN HE WENT DOWN THE DIDEROT BOULEVARD. AN ENORMOUS MAN, BALD, HALF NAKED, AND VERY ANGRY.
I WAS TOLD HE WENT BACK UP VIA NATION AND VANISHED INTO VINCENNES.
EXCUSE ME.
WELL WELL! THE RENEGADE.
BONSOIR, ANDRÉ.
BRETON! I DON'T KNOW WHAT THIS PERSON DID TO DESERVE YOUR CONDEMNATION, BUT I DEMAND THAT YOU INTRODUCE US!
IF I MUST.
RACINE, THIS IS GEORGE SPAD. I PUBLISHED A FEW OF HER AUTOMATIC WRITINGS BEFORE SHE SOLD HER TALENTS TO THE ENEMY.
GEORGE, THIS CHARMING MAN IS RACINE ALFONZO, A BRILLIANT POET PAYING US A VISIT FROM HIS NATIVE MEXICO.
NEITHER BRILLIANT, NOR A POET, BUT MEXICAN, YES!
I LOVE YOUR OUTFIT, MADAME. OR SHOULD I CALL YOU MONSIEUR?
YOU WON'T GET A CHANCE TO.
TAKE THIS, ANDRÉ.

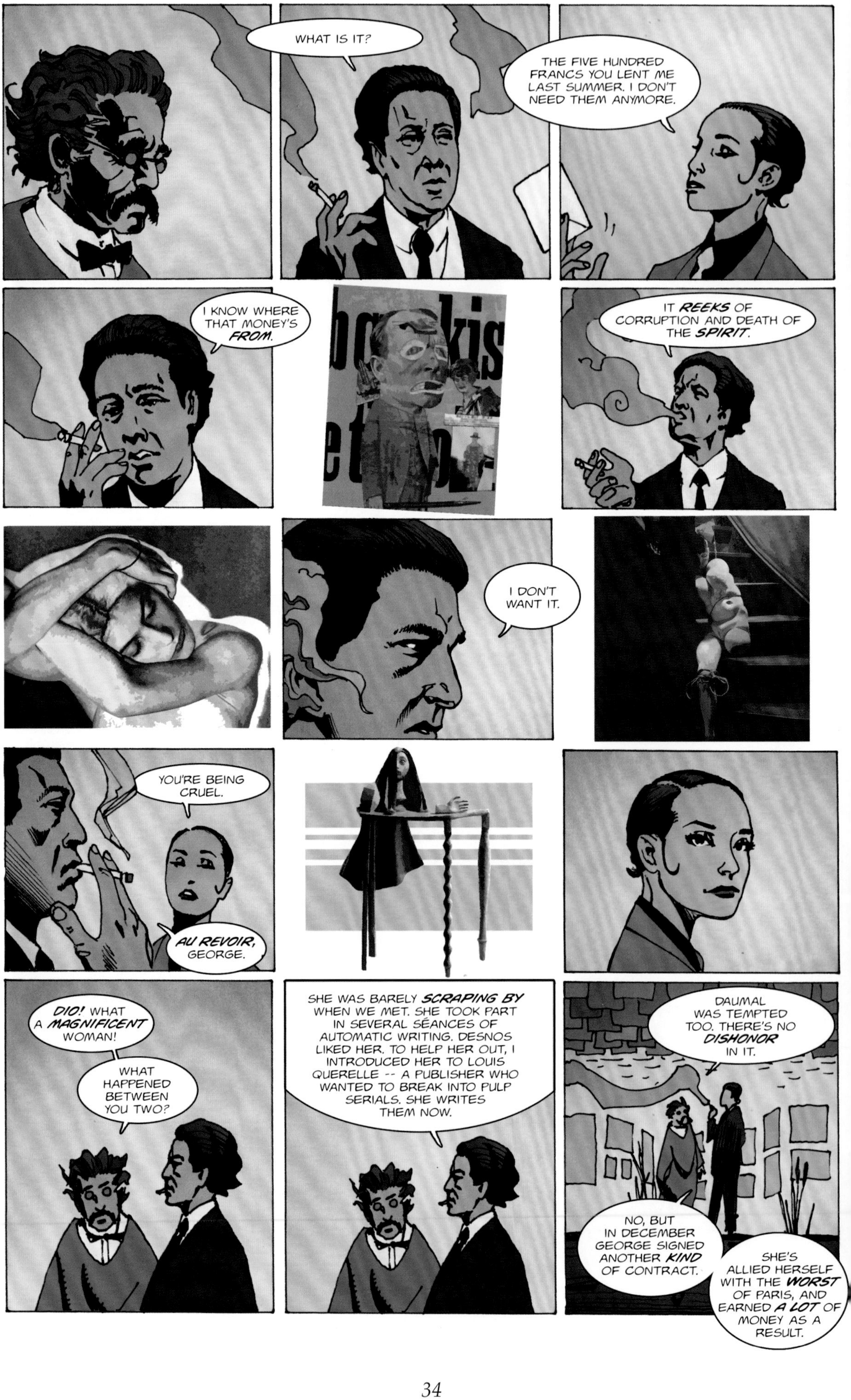
WHAT IS IT?
THE FIVE HUNDRED FRANCS YOU LENT ME LAST SUMMER. I DON'T NEED THEM ANYMORE.
I KNOW WHERE THAT MONEY'S FROM.
IT REEKS OF CORRUPTION AND DEATH OF THE SPIRIT.
I DON'T WANT IT.
YOU'RE BEING CRUEL.
AU REVOIR, GEORGE.
DIO! WHAT A MAGNIFICENT WOMAN!
WHAT HAPPENED BETWEEN YOU TWO?
SHE WAS BARELY SCRAPING BY WHEN WE MET. SHE TOOK PART IN SEVERAL SÉANCES OF AUTOMATIC WRITING. DESNOS LIKED HER. TO HELP HER OUT, I INTRODUCED HER TO LOUIS QUERELLE -- A PUBLISHER WHO WANTED TO BREAK INTO PULP SERIALS. SHE WRITES THEM NOW.
DAUMAL WAS TEMPTED TOO. THERE'S NO DISHONOR IN IT.
NO, BUT IN DECEMBER GEORGE SIGNED ANOTHER KIND OF CONTRACT.
SHE'S ALLIED HERSELF WITH THE WORST OF PARIS, AND EARNED A LOT OF MONEY AS A RESULT.

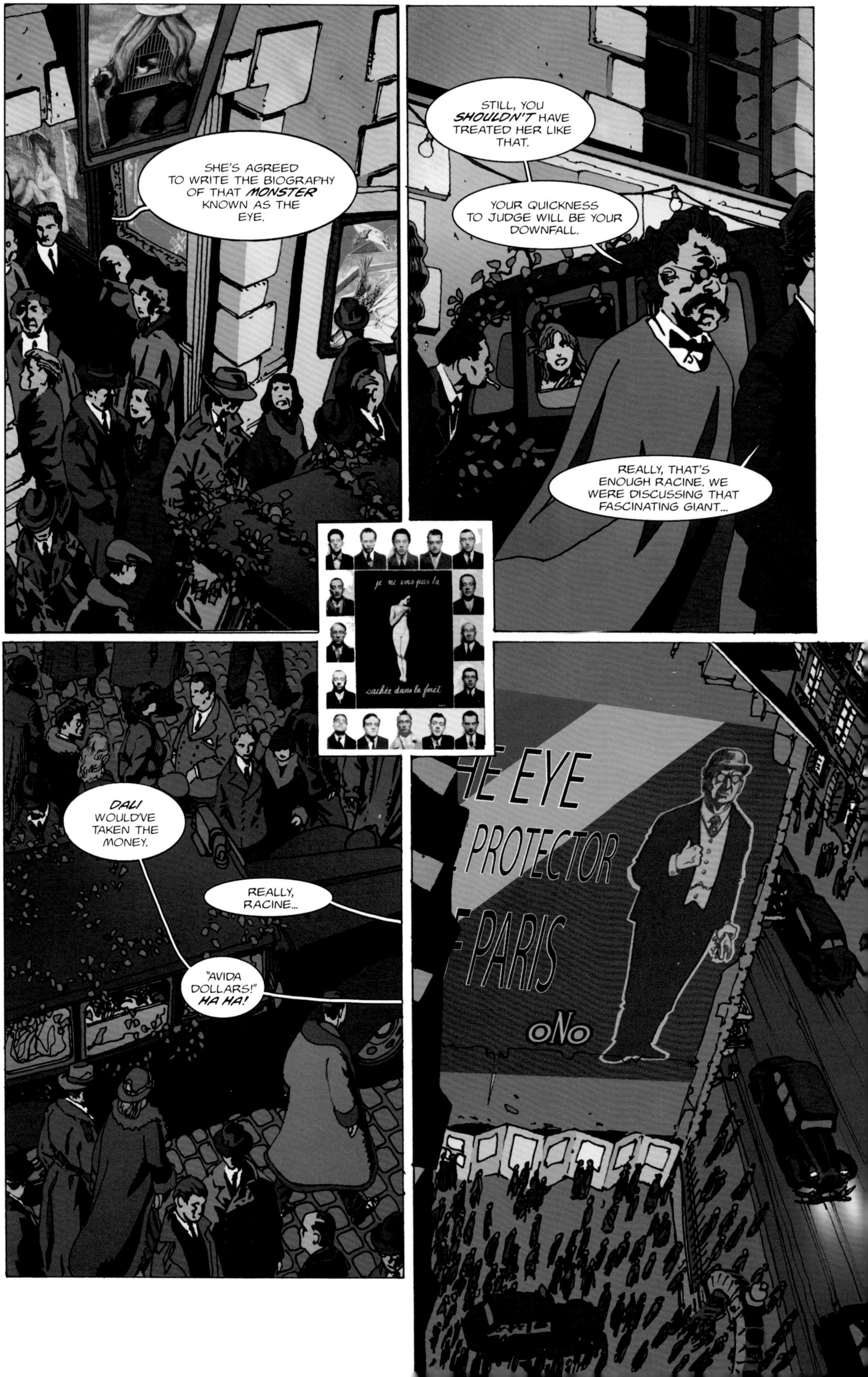
SHE'S AGREED TO WRITE THE BIOGRAPHY OF THAT *MONSTER* KNOWN AS THE EYE.
STILL, YOU *SHOULDN'T* HAVE TREATED HER LIKE THAT.
YOUR QUICKNESS TO JUDGE WILL BE YOUR DOWNFALL.
REALLY, THAT'S ENOUGH RACINE. WE WERE DISCUSSING THAT FASCINATING GIANT...
je ne vois pas la
cachée dans la forêt
DALI WOULD'VE TAKEN THE MONEY.
REALLY, RACINE...
"AVIDA DOLLARS!" *HA HA!*
HE EYE
PROTECTOR
PARIS
oNo

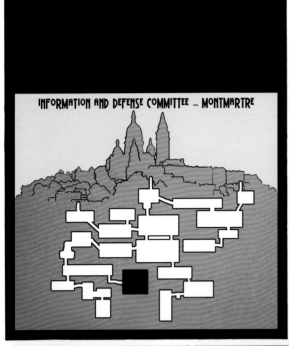

INFORMATION AND DEFENSE COMMITTEE — MONTMARTRE

THE BOSS IS LEAVING.

WHEW.

I...

...JEAN-MARC DUTILLEUL...

...AN EX-BURGLAR...

...ALSO SOMETIMES CALLED "THE SAFECRACKER" AND "THE LONE WOLF"...

...AM KNOWN TODAY THROUGHOUT EUROPE AS "THE MAN WHO WALKS THROUGH WALLS"...

THIS...

...IS MY FINAL MISSION.

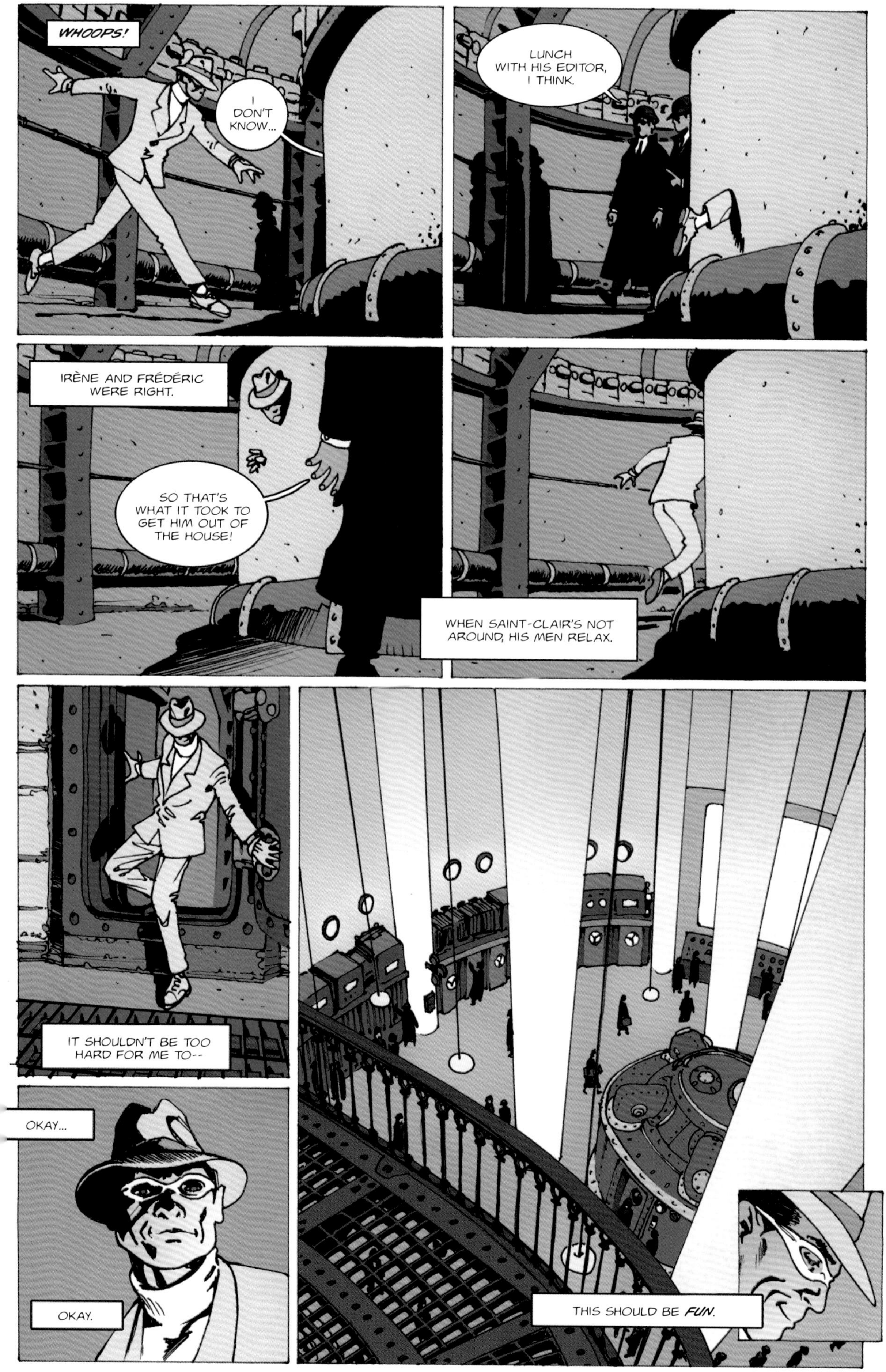
WHOOPS!
I DON'T KNOW...
LUNCH WITH HIS EDITOR, I THINK.
IRÈNE AND FRÉDÉRIC WERE RIGHT.
SO THAT'S WHAT IT TOOK TO GET HIM OUT OF THE HOUSE!
WHEN SAINT-CLAIR'S NOT AROUND, HIS MEN RELAX.
IT SHOULDN'T BE TOO HARD FOR ME TO--
OKAY...
OKAY.
THIS SHOULD BE *FUN*.

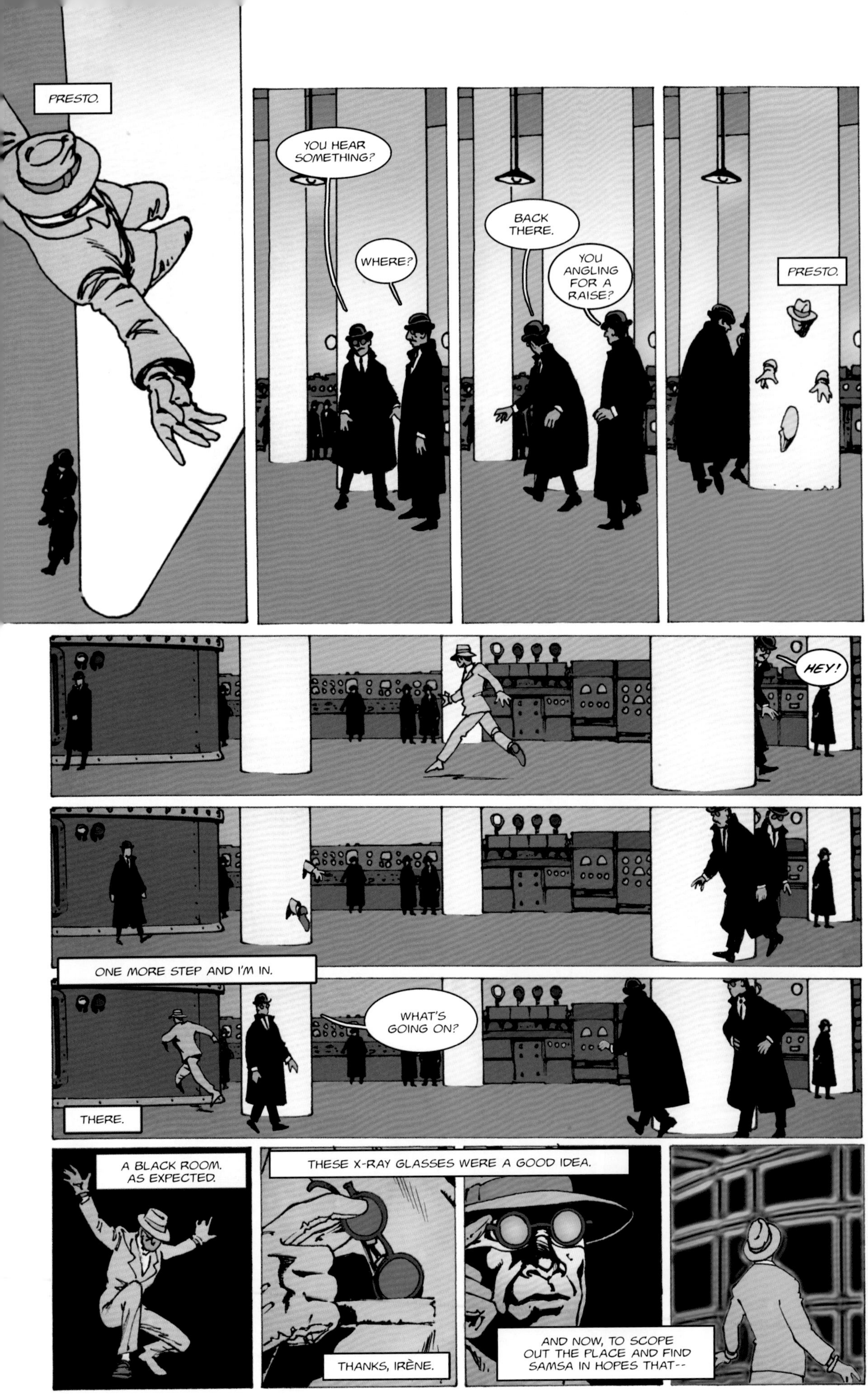
PRESTO.
YOU HEAR SOMETHING?
WHERE?
BACK THERE.
YOU ANGLING FOR A RAISE?
PRESTO.
HEY!
ONE MORE STEP AND I'M IN.
WHAT'S GOING ON?
THERE.
A BLACK ROOM. AS EXPECTED.
THESE X-RAY GLASSES WERE A GOOD IDEA.
THANKS, IRÈNE.
AND NOW, TO SCOPE OUT THE PLACE AND FIND SAMSA IN HOPES THAT--

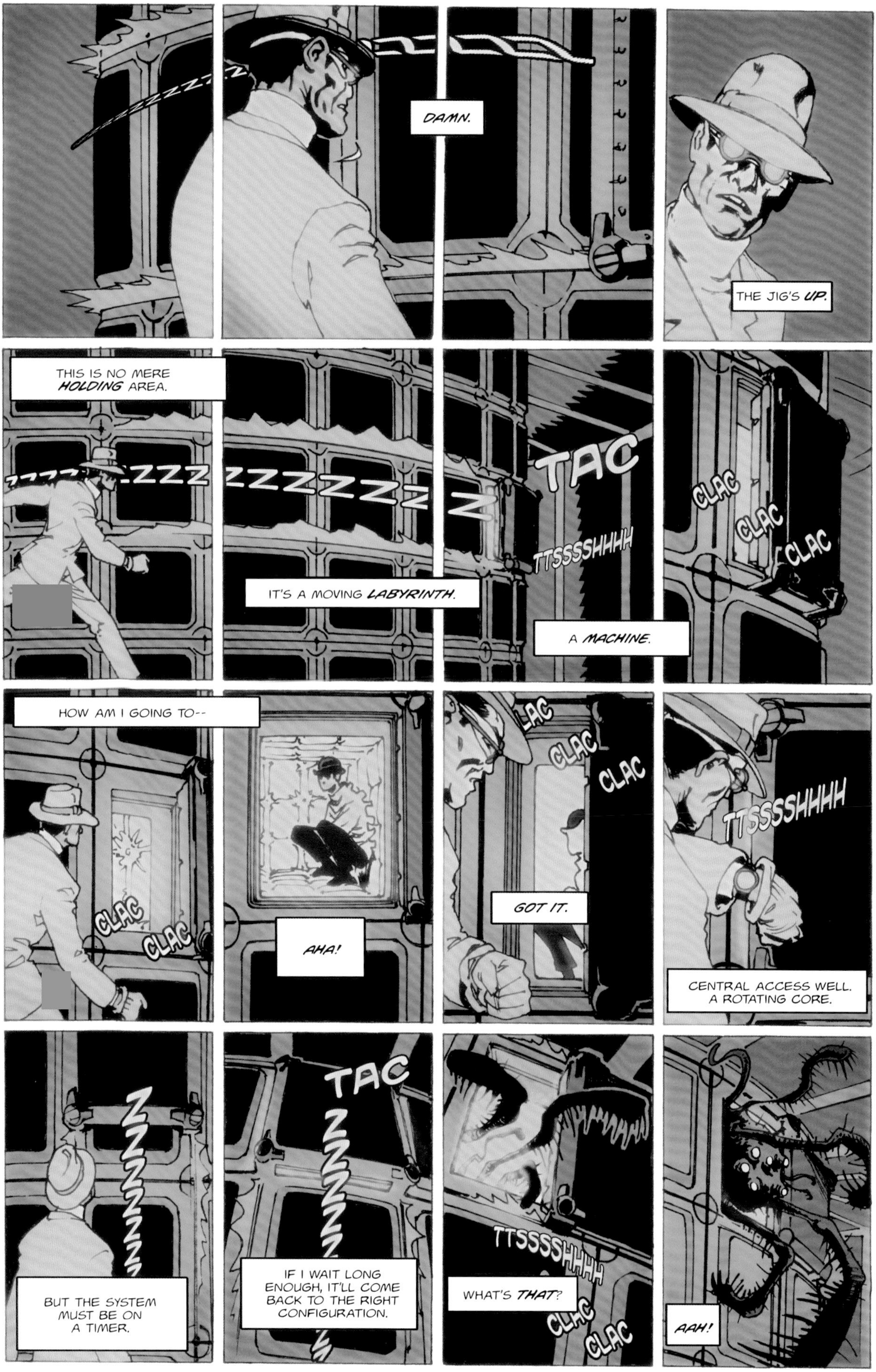
DAMN.
THE JIG'S UP.
THIS IS NO MERE HOLDING AREA.
ZZZZZZZZZZZZZZZZ
IT'S A MOVING LABYRINTH.
TAC
TTSSSSHHHH
A MACHINE.
CLAC
CLAC
CLAC
HOW AM I GOING TO--
CLAC
CLAC
AHA!
CLAC
CLAC
GOT IT.
TTSSSSHHHH
CENTRAL ACCESS WELL. A ROTATING CORE.
BUT THE SYSTEM MUST BE ON A TIMER.
TAC
IF I WAIT LONG ENOUGH, IT'LL COME BACK TO THE RIGHT CONFIGURATION.
TTSSSSHHHH
WHAT'S THAT?
CLAC
CLAC
AAH!

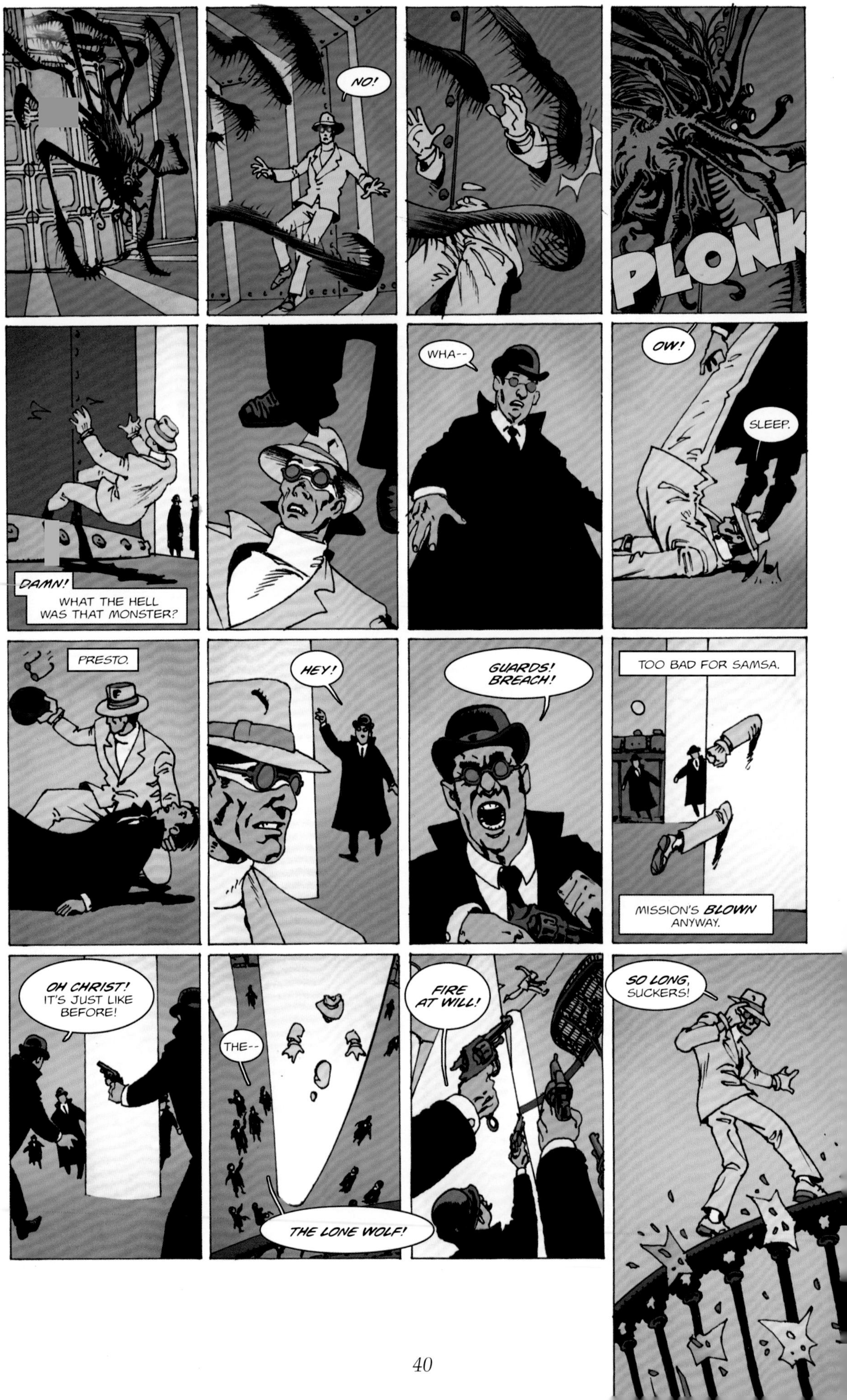
NO!
PLONK
DAMN!
WHAT THE HELL WAS THAT MONSTER?
WHA--
OW!
SLEEP.
PRESTO.
HEY!
GUARDS! BREACH!
TOO BAD FOR SAMSA.
MISSION'S BLOWN ANYWAY.
OH CHRIST! IT'S JUST LIKE BEFORE!
THE--
THE LONE WOLF!
FIRE AT WILL!
SO LONG, SUCKERS!

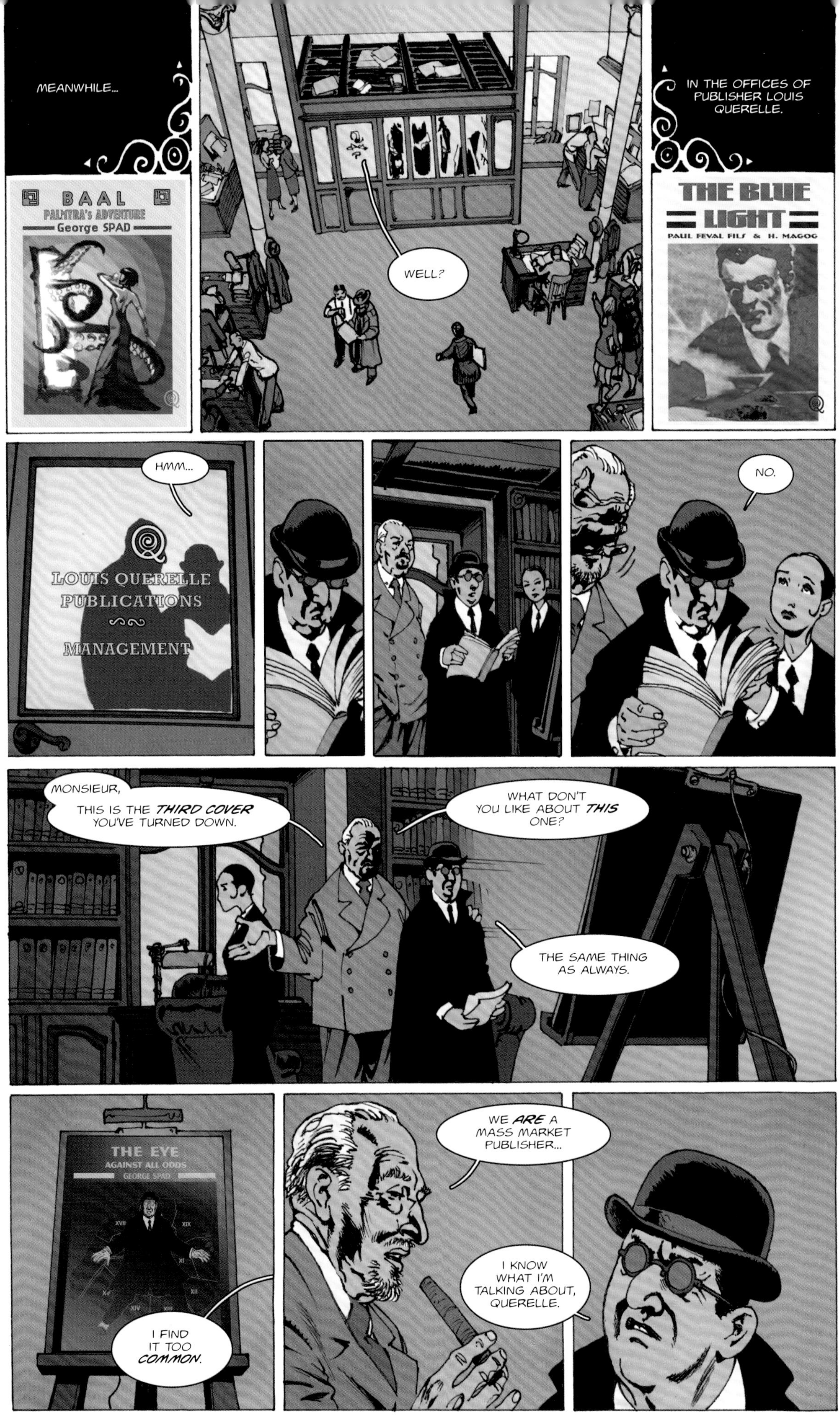
MEANWHILE...
IN THE OFFICES OF PUBLISHER LOUIS QUERELLE.
BAAL
PALMYRA's ADVENTURE
George SPAD
WELL?
THE BLUE LIGHT
PAUL FEVAL FILS & H. MAGOG
HMM...
LOUIS QUERELLE PUBLICATIONS
MANAGEMENT
NO.
MONSIEUR,
THIS IS THE *THIRD COVER* YOU'VE TURNED DOWN.
WHAT DON'T YOU LIKE ABOUT *THIS* ONE?
THE SAME THING AS ALWAYS.
THE EYE
AGAINST ALL ODDS
GEORGE SPAD
I FIND IT TOO *COMMON*.
WE *ARE* A MASS MARKET PUBLISHER...
I KNOW WHAT I'M TALKING ABOUT, QUERELLE.

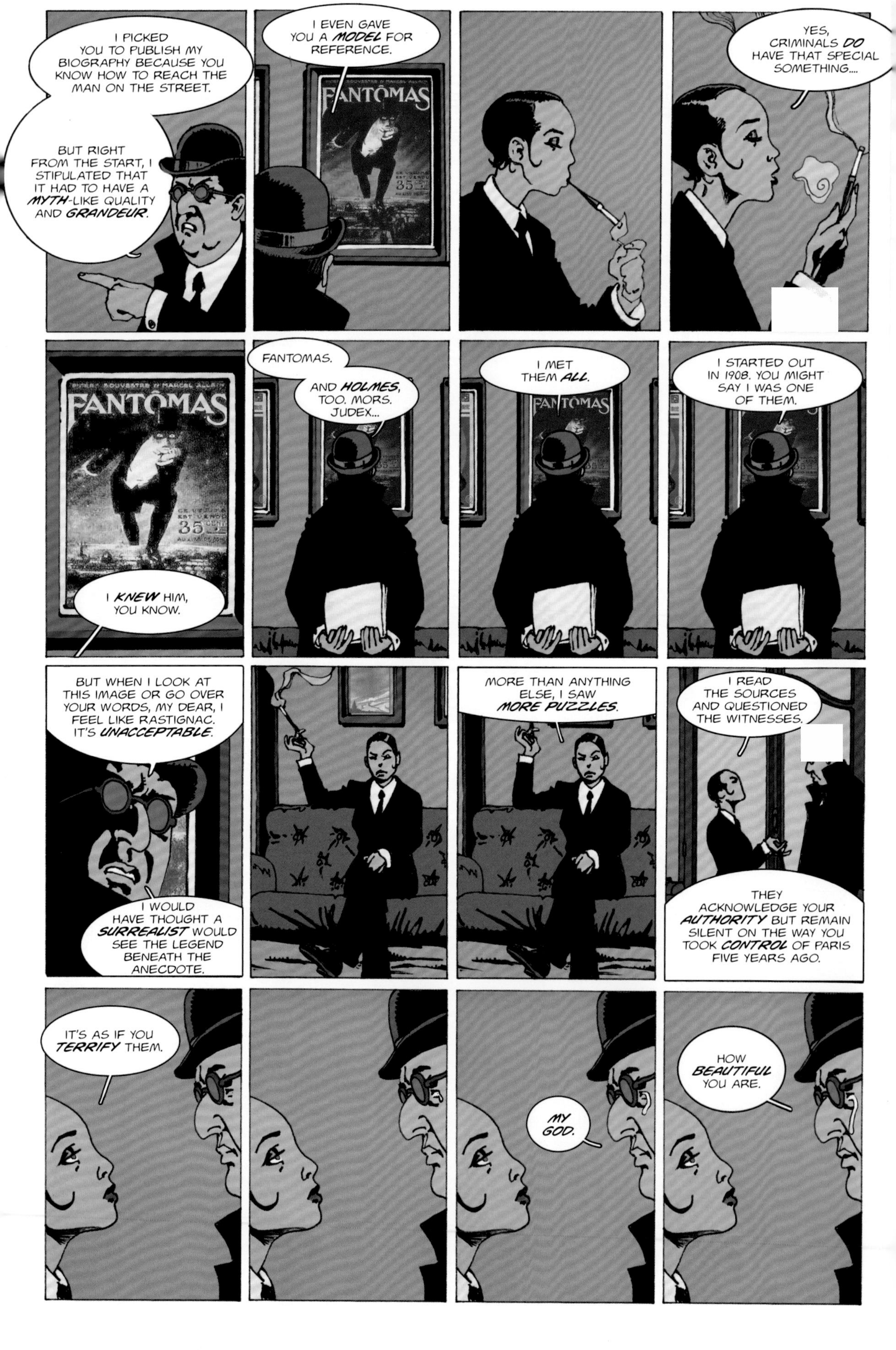
I PICKED YOU TO PUBLISH MY BIOGRAPHY BECAUSE YOU KNOW HOW TO REACH THE MAN ON THE STREET.
BUT RIGHT FROM THE START, I STIPULATED THAT IT HAD TO HAVE A MYTH-LIKE QUALITY AND GRANDEUR.
I EVEN GAVE YOU A MODEL FOR REFERENCE.
FANTÔMAS
YES, CRIMINALS DO HAVE THAT SPECIAL SOMETHING....
FANTÔMAS
35
I KNEW HIM, YOU KNOW.
FANTOMAS.
AND HOLMES, TOO. MORS. JUDEX...
I MET THEM ALL.
I STARTED OUT IN 1908. YOU MIGHT SAY I WAS ONE OF THEM.
BUT WHEN I LOOK AT THIS IMAGE OR GO OVER YOUR WORDS, MY DEAR, I FEEL LIKE RASTIGNAC. IT'S UNACCEPTABLE.
I WOULD HAVE THOUGHT A SURREALIST WOULD SEE THE LEGEND BENEATH THE ANECDOTE.
MORE THAN ANYTHING ELSE, I SAW MORE PUZZLES.
I READ THE SOURCES AND QUESTIONED THE WITNESSES.
THEY ACKNOWLEDGE YOUR AUTHORITY BUT REMAIN SILENT ON THE WAY YOU TOOK CONTROL OF PARIS FIVE YEARS AGO.
IT'S AS IF YOU TERRIFY THEM.
MY GOD.
HOW BEAUTIFUL YOU ARE.

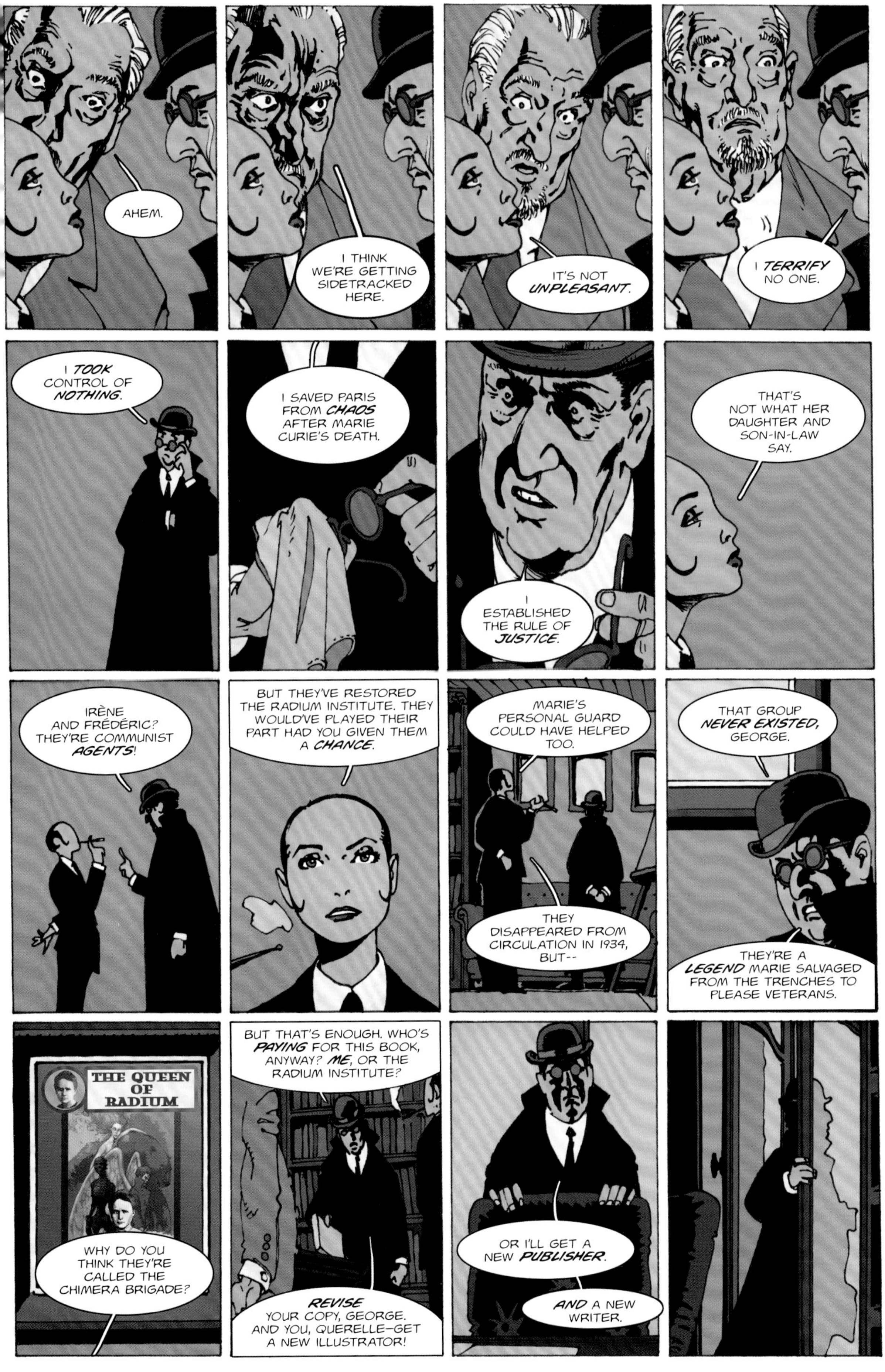
AHEM.
I THINK WE'RE GETTING SIDETRACKED HERE.
IT'S NOT UNPLEASANT.
I TERRIFY NO ONE.
I TOOK CONTROL OF NOTHING.
I SAVED PARIS FROM CHAOS AFTER MARIE CURIE'S DEATH.
I ESTABLISHED THE RULE OF JUSTICE.
THAT'S NOT WHAT HER DAUGHTER AND SON-IN-LAW SAY.
IRÈNE AND FRÉDÉRIC? THEY'RE COMMUNIST AGENTS!
BUT THEY'VE RESTORED THE RADIUM INSTITUTE. THEY WOULD'VE PLAYED THEIR PART HAD YOU GIVEN THEM A CHANCE.
MARIE'S PERSONAL GUARD COULD HAVE HELPED TOO.
THEY DISAPPEARED FROM CIRCULATION IN 1934, BUT--
THAT GROUP NEVER EXISTED, GEORGE.
THEY'RE A LEGEND MARIE SALVAGED FROM THE TRENCHES TO PLEASE VETERANS.
THE QUEEN OF RADIUM
WHY DO YOU THINK THEY'RE CALLED THE CHIMERA BRIGADE?
BUT THAT'S ENOUGH. WHO'S PAYING FOR THIS BOOK, ANYWAY? ME, OR THE RADIUM INSTITUTE?
REVISE YOUR COPY, GEORGE. AND YOU, QUERELLE—GET A NEW ILLUSTRATOR!
OR I'LL GET A NEW PUBLISHER.
AND A NEW WRITER.

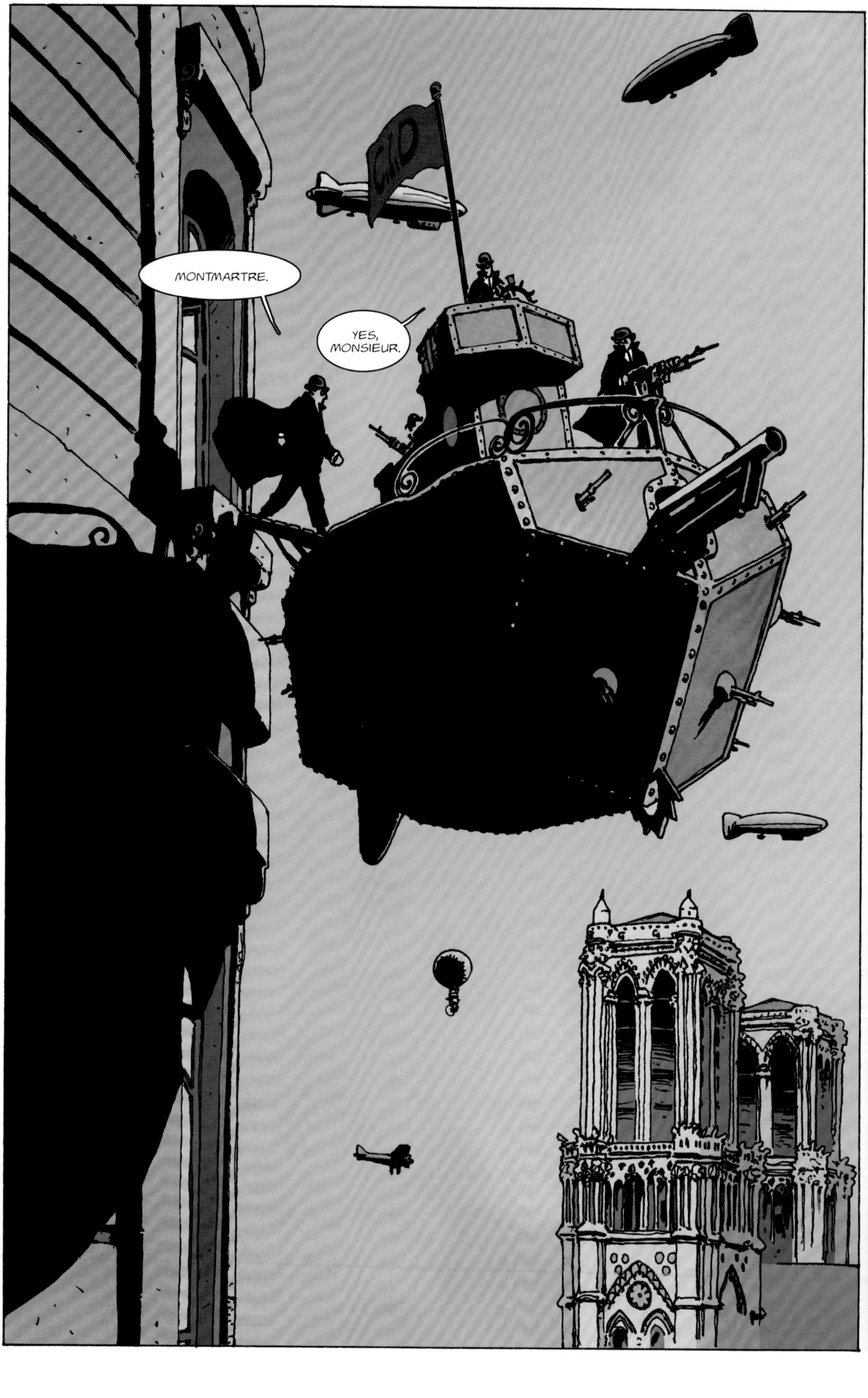
MONTMARTRE.
YES, MONSIEUR.

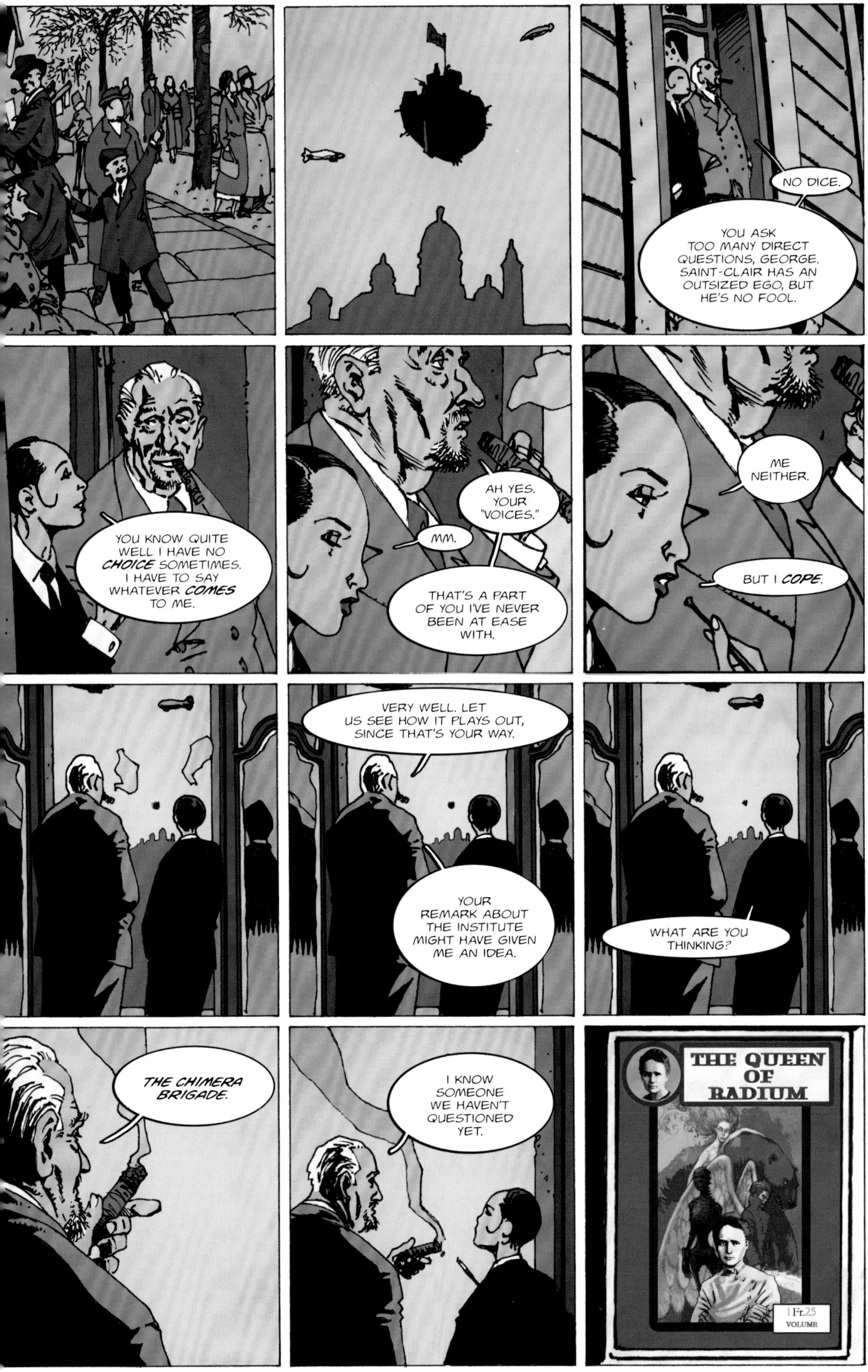
NO DICE.
YOU ASK TOO MANY DIRECT QUESTIONS, GEORGE. SAINT-CLAIR HAS AN OUTSIZED EGO, BUT HE'S NO FOOL.
YOU KNOW QUITE WELL I HAVE NO CHOICE SOMETIMES. I HAVE TO SAY WHATEVER COMES TO ME.
MM.
AH YES. YOUR "VOICES."
THAT'S A PART OF YOU I'VE NEVER BEEN AT EASE WITH.
ME NEITHER.
BUT I COPE.
VERY WELL. LET US SEE HOW IT PLAYS OUT, SINCE THAT'S YOUR WAY.
YOUR REMARK ABOUT THE INSTITUTE MIGHT HAVE GIVEN ME AN IDEA.
WHAT ARE YOU THINKING?
THE CHIMERA BRIGADE.
I KNOW SOMEONE WE HAVEN'T QUESTIONED YET.
THE QUEEN OF RADIUM
1 Fr.25
VOLUME

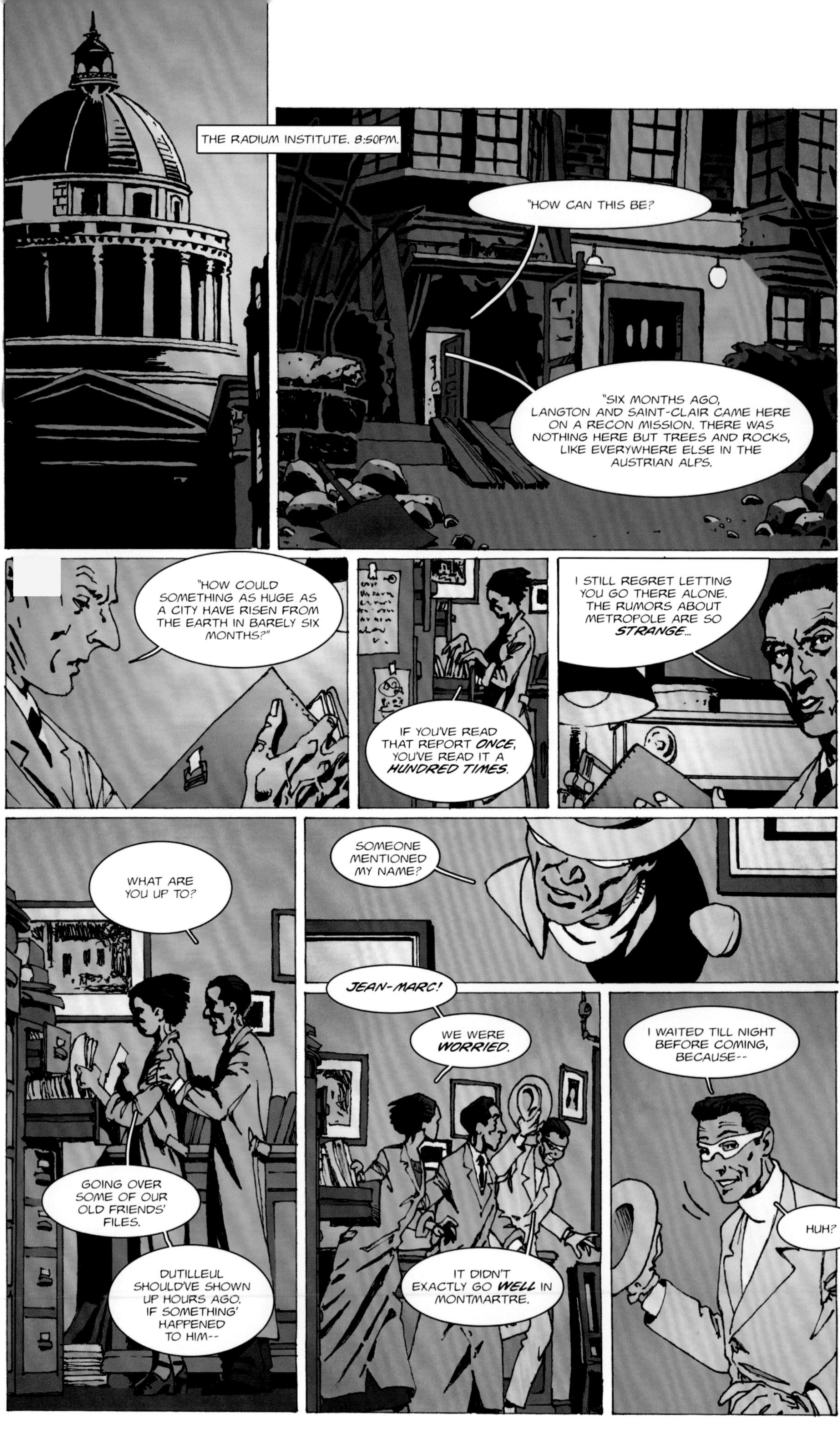
THE RADIUM INSTITUTE. 8:50PM.
"HOW CAN THIS BE?
"SIX MONTHS AGO, LANGTON AND SAINT-CLAIR CAME HERE ON A RECON MISSION. THERE WAS NOTHING HERE BUT TREES AND ROCKS, LIKE EVERYWHERE ELSE IN THE AUSTRIAN ALPS.
"HOW COULD SOMETHING AS HUGE AS A CITY HAVE RISEN FROM THE EARTH IN BARELY SIX MONTHS?"
IF YOU'VE READ THAT REPORT ONCE, YOU'VE READ IT A HUNDRED TIMES.
I STILL REGRET LETTING YOU GO THERE ALONE. THE RUMORS ABOUT METROPOLE ARE SO STRANGE...
WHAT ARE YOU UP TO?
GOING OVER SOME OF OUR OLD FRIENDS' FILES.
DUTILLEUL SHOULD'VE SHOWN UP HOURS AGO. IF SOMETHING' HAPPENED TO HIM--
SOMEONE MENTIONED MY NAME?
JEAN-MARC!
WE WERE WORRIED.
IT DIDN'T EXACTLY GO WELL IN MONTMARTRE.
I WAITED TILL NIGHT BEFORE COMING, BECAUSE--
HUH?

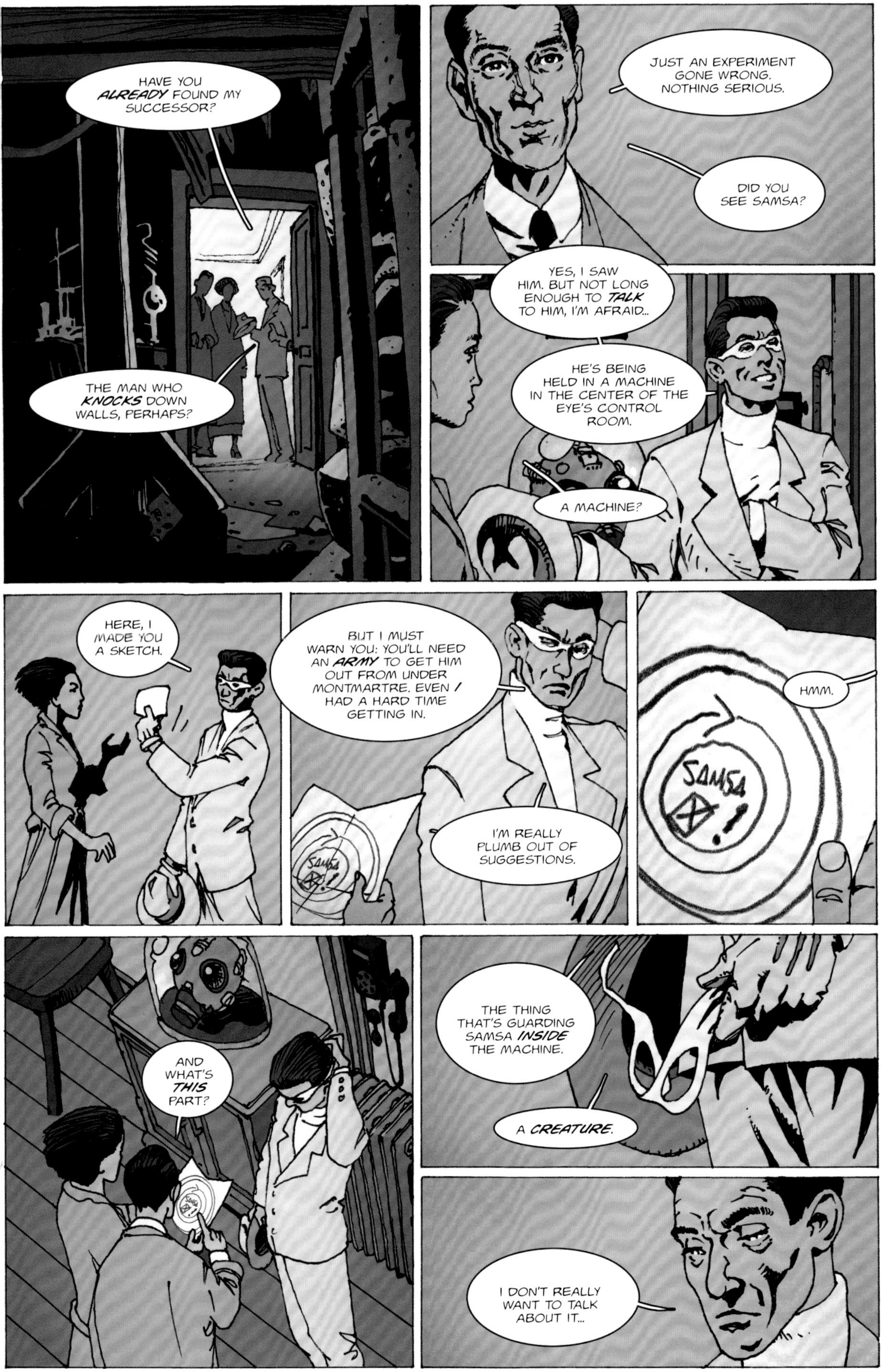
HAVE YOU *ALREADY* FOUND MY SUCCESSOR?
THE MAN WHO *KNOCKS* DOWN WALLS, PERHAPS?
JUST AN EXPERIMENT GONE WRONG. NOTHING SERIOUS.
DID YOU SEE SAMSA?
YES, I SAW HIM. BUT NOT LONG ENOUGH TO *TALK* TO HIM, I'M AFRAID...
HE'S BEING HELD IN A MACHINE IN THE CENTER OF THE EYE'S CONTROL ROOM.
A MACHINE?
HERE, I MADE YOU A SKETCH.
BUT I MUST WARN YOU: YOU'LL NEED AN *ARMY* TO GET HIM OUT FROM UNDER MONTMARTRE. EVEN *I* HAD A HARD TIME GETTING IN.
I'M REALLY PLUMB OUT OF SUGGESTIONS.
HMM.
SAMSA
AND WHAT'S *THIS* PART?
THE THING THAT'S GUARDING SAMSA *INSIDE* THE MACHINE.
A *CREATURE*.
I DON'T REALLY WANT TO TALK ABOUT IT...

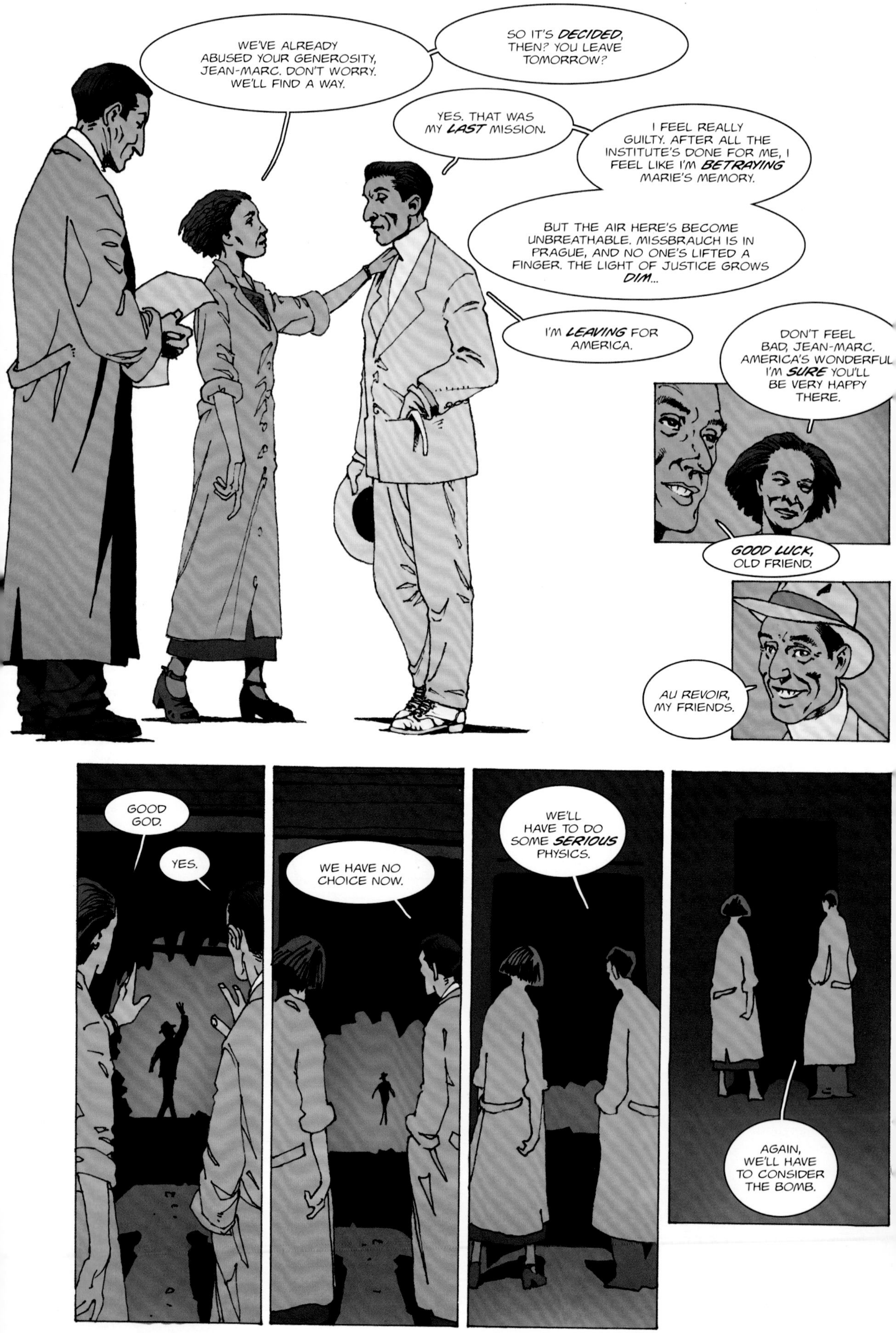
WE'VE ALREADY ABUSED YOUR GENEROSITY, JEAN-MARC. DON'T WORRY. WE'LL FIND A WAY.
SO IT'S DECIDED, THEN? YOU LEAVE TOMORROW?
YES. THAT WAS MY LAST MISSION.
I FEEL REALLY GUILTY. AFTER ALL THE INSTITUTE'S DONE FOR ME, I FEEL LIKE I'M BETRAYING MARIE'S MEMORY.
BUT THE AIR HERE'S BECOME UNBREATHABLE. MISSBRAUCH IS IN PRAGUE, AND NO ONE'S LIFTED A FINGER. THE LIGHT OF JUSTICE GROWS DIM...
I'M LEAVING FOR AMERICA.
DON'T FEEL BAD, JEAN-MARC. AMERICA'S WONDERFUL. I'M SURE YOU'LL BE VERY HAPPY THERE.
GOOD LUCK, OLD FRIEND.
AU REVOIR, MY FRIENDS.
GOOD GOD.
YES.
WE HAVE NO CHOICE NOW.
WE'LL HAVE TO DO SOME SERIOUS PHYSICS.
AGAIN, WE'LL HAVE TO CONSIDER THE BOMB.

NEXT EPISODE:
CAGLIOSTRO!

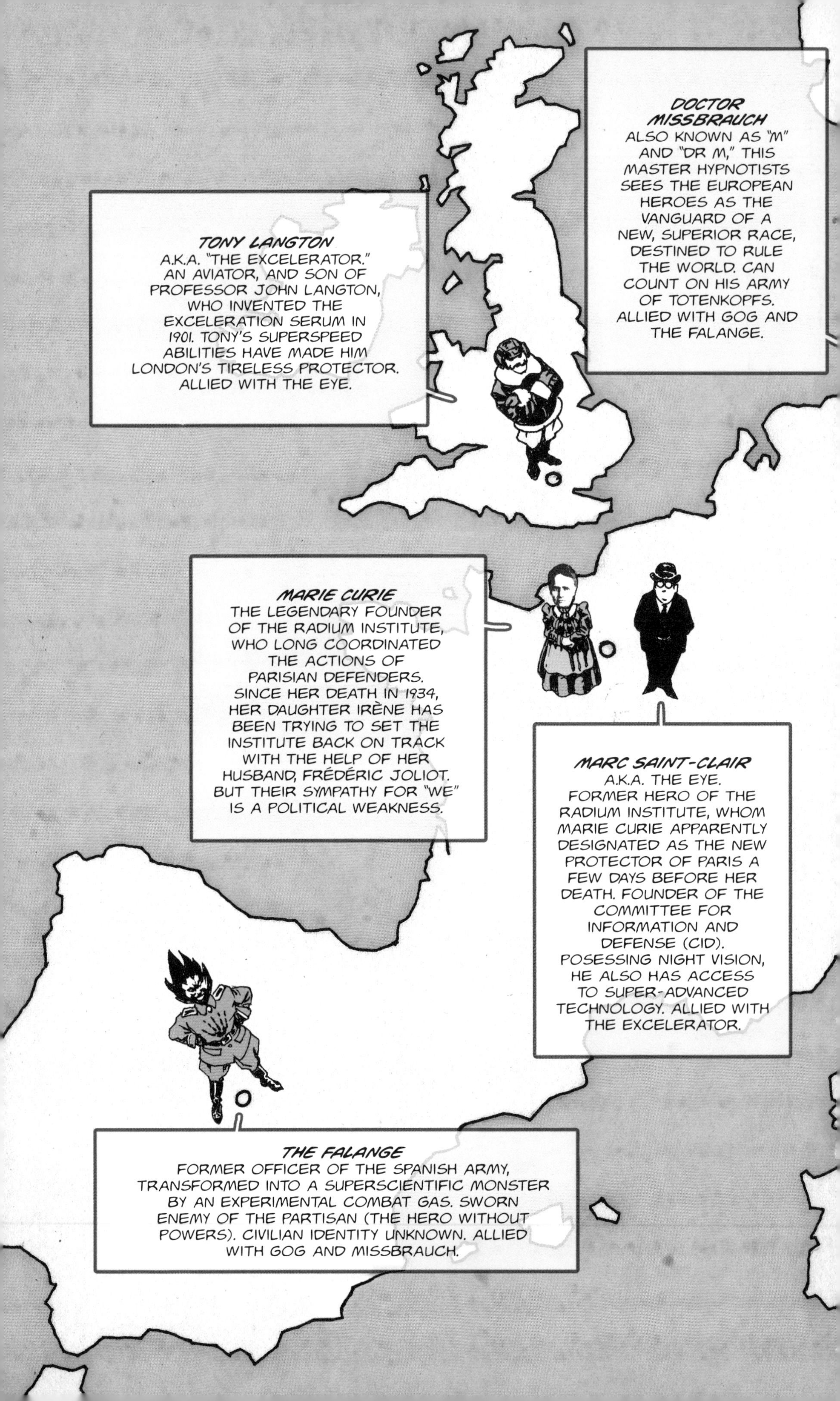
DOCTOR MISSBRAUCH
ALSO KNOWN AS "M" AND "DR M," THIS MASTER HYPNOTISTS SEES THE EUROPEAN HEROES AS THE VANGUARD OF A NEW, SUPERIOR RACE, DESTINED TO RULE THE WORLD. CAN COUNT ON HIS ARMY OF TOTENKOPFS. ALLIED WITH GOG AND THE FALANGE.
TONY LANGTON
A.K.A. "THE EXCELERATOR." AN AVIATOR, AND SON OF PROFESSOR JOHN LANGTON, WHO INVENTED THE EXCELERATION SERUM IN 1901. TONY'S SUPERSPEED ABILITIES HAVE MADE HIM LONDON'S TIRELESS PROTECTOR. ALLIED WITH THE EYE.
MARIE CURIE
THE LEGENDARY FOUNDER OF THE RADIUM INSTITUTE, WHO LONG COORDINATED THE ACTIONS OF PARISIAN DEFENDERS. SINCE HER DEATH IN 1934, HER DAUGHTER IRÈNE HAS BEEN TRYING TO SET THE INSTITUTE BACK ON TRACK WITH THE HELP OF HER HUSBAND, FRÉDÉRIC JOLIOT. BUT THEIR SYMPATHY FOR "WE" IS A POLITICAL WEAKNESS.
MARC SAINT-CLAIR
A.K.A. THE EYE. FORMER HERO OF THE RADIUM INSTITUTE, WHOM MARIE CURIE APPARENTLY DESIGNATED AS THE NEW PROTECTOR OF PARIS A FEW DAYS BEFORE HER DEATH. FOUNDER OF THE COMMITTEE FOR INFORMATION AND DEFENSE (CID). POSESSING NIGHT VISION, HE ALSO HAS ACCESS TO SUPER-ADVANCED TECHNOLOGY. ALLIED WITH THE EXCELERATOR.
THE FALANGE
FORMER OFFICER OF THE SPANISH ARMY, TRANSFORMED INTO A SUPERSCIENTIFIC MONSTER BY AN EXPERIMENTAL COMBAT GAS. SWORN ENEMY OF THE PARTISAN (THE HERO WITHOUT POWERS). CIVILIAN IDENTITY UNKNOWN. ALLIED WITH GOG AND MISSBRAUCH.